5/2/12
8/15

P9-CNC-667

THE
DOORS

ALSO BY GREIL MARCUS

Mystery Train: Images of America in Rock 'n' Roll Music (1975, 2008)

Lipstick Traces: A Secret History of the 20th Century (1989, 2009)

Dead Elvis: A Chronicle of a Cultural Obsession (1991)

In the Fascist Bathroom: Punk in Pop Music, 1977–92
(1993, originally published as *Ranters & Crowd Pleasers*)

The Dustbin of History (1995)

The Old, Weird America: The World of Bob Dylan's Basement Tapes
(2000, 2011, originally published as *Invisible Republic*, 1997)

*Double Trouble: Bill Clinton and Elvis Presley in a Land
of No Alternatives* (2000)

"The Manchurian Candidate" (2002)

Like a Rolling Stone: Bob Dylan at the Crossroads (2005)

The Shape of Things to Come: Prophecy and the American Voice (2006)

When that Rough God Goes Riding: Listening to Van Morrison (2010)

Bob Dylan by Greil Marcus, Writings 1968–2010 (2010)

AS EDITOR

Stranded (1979, 2007)

Psychotic Reactions & Carburetor Dung by Lester Bangs (1987)

The Rose & the Briar: Death, Love and Liberty in the American Ballad
(2004, with Sean Wilentz)

Best Music Writing 2009 (2009)

A New Literary History of America (2009, with Werner Sollors)

THE
DOORS

A Lifetime of Listening to Five Mean Years

Greil Marcus

PublicAffairs
New York

Editorial production by Marrathon Production Services. www.marrathon.net

BOOK DESIGN BY JANE RAESE
Text set in 11.5-point Electra

The Library of Congress has cataloged the printed edition as follows:
Marcus, Greil.
The Doors : a lifetime of listening to five mean years / Greil Marcus. — 1st ed.
p. cm.
1. Doors (Musical group) 2. Rock music—1961–1970—History and criticism.
I. Title.
ML421.D66M38   2011
782.42166092'2—dc23
2011027931

ISBN 978-1-58648-945-8 (hardcover)
ISBN 978-1-58648-946-5 (e-Book)

FIRST EDITION

10 9 8 7 6 5 4 3 2 1

TO LARRY MILLER

CONTENTS

THE DOORS—Ray Manzarek, born 1939, Jim Morrison, 1943, John Densmore, 1944, and Robby Krieger, 1946—formed in Venice, a Southern California beach town, in 1965. They started out at parties, weddings, and high-school proms, and played their last show on December 12, 1970, at the Warehouse in New Orleans. Jim Morrison died in Paris on July 3, 1971.

JIM MORRISON: "Interviews are good, but . . ."

GREG SHAW: "Oh, they're a drag."

JIM MORRISON: "Critical essays are really where it's at."

—"Interview with the Doors,"
Mojo Navigator Rock + Roll News
no. 14, August 1967

Prologue:
Light My Fire, 1967

BY SEPTEMBER 30, 1967, when the Doors appeared at the Family Dog in Denver—an outpost of the Avalon Ballroom in San Francisco, where the band had played often in the first months of the year—"Light My Fire" had already reached number one all over the country. In fact it had stolen the year, at first the nearly seven minutes of the song creeping out of the night on the few, new FM rock 'n' roll stations that still seemed more rumor than fact, then in a cut-down, three-minute version taking over AM Top 40 stations everywhere, sending their listeners into the record stores or in search of FM if they could find it, to hear the whole song, or to the phones to demand that the AM disc jockeys play it all, which soon enough they did.

This night in Denver it was a fair bet that everyone in the hall had already heard the thing at least four or five hundred times. The Doors had already played it for more than a year, from the nowhere London Fog club off Sunset Strip in Los Angeles to the celebrated Whisky à Go Go on it and at every show after that. They played it before anyone had heard of them; they played it until well after the name of the band was on so many lips that, more than forty years past the singer's death, after he had been dead for far more years than he had been alive, the name of the band still struck a chord. It wasn't a chord of memory. It was a note of possibility, of promises made that still remained to be kept, promises that in life were inevitably failed and in the music left behind were kept over and over again.

"We really didn't see it coming, the new world of rabid individualism and the sanctity of profit," the British novelist Jenny Diski wrote in 2009. "But perhaps that is only to be expected. It's possible after all that we were simply young, and now we are simply old and looking back as every generation does nostalgically to our best of times. Perhaps the Sixties are an idea that has had its day and lingers long after its time. Except, of course, for the music."

There were, of course, those, the great majority, doubtless, who, having finished with their wild youth, put on proper suits come the mid-Seventies and went off to work and a regular life, becoming all their parents could have wished, having just gone through a phase, as the more liberal of the grown-ups had always suggested. But some—these days called, derogatorily, idealists—maintained their former sense that "society" exists, and believe it persists, even beyond the strident years of

Margaret Thatcher and the official approved decades of self-interest and greed that have followed. We are the disappointed remnant, the rump of the Sixties.

But that drama was already taking place only two months after "Light My Fire" hit the top of the charts.

How do we make this song into something they haven't heard before? How do we make it into something we haven't heard before?

On September 30 there's a lift in Jim Morrison's voice for the first two times he reaches the word *fire* in each chorus, as if running his hands over the single syllable—always, he communicates that as an idea that word is new to him, and so it comes across as a surprise. You've heard the word in the song, but you haven't begun to follow that fire as far as it goes—that's the feeling. "Fire"—it's a door swinging open in the wind, seen from a distance.

Compared to the first two times the word is sung on record, the third time—"FY-YUR!"—is vulgar, a hook, something to wake you up if the song has already put you to sleep. But tonight, in the first chorus, Morrison stays with the word as he first sang it: *Fire . . . fiiire . . . fiiiiire.* He holds the word up to the light, looking at it from all sides, still letting it float in the air. "Light my fire" was already a cliché, a tired catchphrase by September; within a year it would be a teen-sex poster and a worldwide easy-listening hit by Jose Feliciano, in two years a porn movie. Now, as the song starts, the word *fire* seems like a strange thing to say, less a word than a rayograph.

The recording from this night is from a bootleg, the sound squeezed into itself. Robby Krieger's guitar and Ray Manzarek's organ can seem like the same instrument. But John

Densmore's drumming is always defined, each beat feeling like a choice made, sealed, and left behind. Morrison's voice floats over the band, even when he seems to be shouting from far behind it—shouting encouragement, as if the song as it builds isn't enough, isn't yet itself—

COME ON!
LET'S GO!

—then as Manzarek hits a momentum that carries him into the song Morrison is pushing him toward, celebrating that the song is whole, breathing its own air—

LET'S GO!
WE LOVE IT!

—then drifting away, as if the music no longer needs him to tell it what to do—

In your night, babe
Evil hand

But the long instrumental passages, handed back and forth between Manzarek and Krieger, are hard to hold on to. They're meanders, what Manny Faber, talking about painting, talking about movies, talking about jazz, called termite art, art that "feels its way through walls of particularization, with no sign that the artist has any object in mind other than eating away the immediate boundaries of his art, and turning these boundaries into conditions of the next achievement." It's art without intent, without thinking, art by desire, appetite, instinct, and impulse, and it can as easily meander in circles as cross borders and leap gaps. This night Manzarek and Krieger lose the song, as if they've forgotten what they were playing. For a moment "Light My Fire" disappears, as if it's never been performed before, as if there's no referent, no hit that was ever on the radio. As it will do so many times in the next three years, the song devolves back into other songs, songs that edge out of the vague memory of one musician or another and replace the song they were playing a minute before; this time it's "My Favorite Things," a cool jazz moment in a performance that's no longer part of a rock 'n' roll show in Denver but back in the Venice beach house where the song was found, though now it's not 1965 but 1954 and the person everyone's looking at isn't Jim Morrison but Chet Baker.

They lose the beat, the song slips, they have trouble finding their way back into the verses, stumbling over the steps back into the fanfare that opens the song, that closes it, that marks Morrison's stride back into the music, that tells you something is about to happen, that makes it clear something has.

It's a relief when Morrison is back at the center, when there are words to attack, when there's a song to take back and rebuild, on the spot; at seven minutes and fifteen seconds into the song it's a thrill. But the song isn't there for Morrison either. The hundreds of thousands of times the song has been broadcast on the radio without the solos the musicians have just found and lost have left the song without a body, just head, hands, and feet, spinning, flailing.

Densmore brings it back, with one single hard shuffle that breaks a line between the verse, with its bad rhyme of "mire" and "pyre," and the chorus, a pattern of five strokes that says, *Time's up. Put up or shut up.* And that does it: for the first time, the song is absolutely present, an event taking place as you listen. For the last minute of the performance, the sense of will and strain is so strong that Morrison might be down on his knees, pushing the song through a wall. Every time Densmore leaps to the front of the sound, the certainty that the song will break through is overwhelming; in the next instant, when Morrison takes Densmore's place, desperation builds on itself. Now it's Manzarek who's shouting from behind, all excitement—

ALL RIGHT!

—then with excitement wrapped in fright—

GO!

—fright that the wall may hold, that for all that Morrison puts into "Try to set the night on fire," it won't happen.

When the song finally crashes to a close, you can't tell if it happened or not. As the song ends they're still pushing, the wall is still holding. The song is over but the story it's telling is still going on. You can't hear it but you can feel it on your skin.

Jenny Diski, *The Sixties* (New York: Picador, 2009), 9, 87.

"Light My Fire," Family Dog, Denver, September 30, 1967, from *Boot Yer Butt! The Doors Bootlegs*, a collection of audience and fans' concert recordings (Rhino Handmade, 2003).

Manny Farber, "White Elephant Art vs. Termite Art," *Film Culture*, 1962. Collected in *Farber on Film: The Complete Film Writings of Manny Farber* (New York: Library of America, 2003), 535.

Come On Baby, Light My Fire, directed by Lou Campa (J. R. L. Productions, 1969). According to Movies Unlimited, "A goody two-shoes anti-marijuana campaigner [Tina Buckley] is abducted by a group of perverts who take her to the home of a drug kingpin, played by Gerard Damiano of 'Deep Throat' fame. Soon, the doors of submission and domination are opened when she's forced to become their sex slave."

L.A. Woman

A s the title track of the Doors last album, released in April 1971, three months before Jim Morrison died in Paris, his ideal of following in the footsteps of Rimbaud replaced by an image of Marat dead in his bathtub, "L.A. Woman" emerged over the years, until after four decades you could turn on your car radio and find all eight minutes of it still talking, jabbering, this bum on Sunset Strip going on about a woman and the city and the night as if someone other than himself is actually listening. You can hear it there, anytime—and you can hear it playing between every other line of Thomas Pynchon's 2009 L.A. detective novel *Inherent Vice*, set in the spring of 1970, just before the Manson trial is about to begin, a time when, as Pynchon calls it up, the freeways eastbound from the beach towns "teemed with VW buses in jittering paisleys, primer-coated street hemis, woodies of authentic Dearborn pine, TV-star-piloted Porsches, Cadillacs carrying dentists to extramarital trysts, windowless vans with lurid teen dramas in progress inside, pickups with mattresses full of country cousins from the San Joaquin, all wheeling along together down into these great horizonless fields of housing, under the power transmission lines, everybody's radios lasing on the same couple of AM stations."

The book is a love letter to a time and place about to vanish: about the fear that "the Psychedelic Sixties, this little parenthesis of light, might close after all, and all be lost, taken back into darkness . . . how a certain hand might reach terribly out of darkness and reclaim the time, easy as taking a joint from a doper and stubbing it out for good."

At the very time in which Pynchon has placed his story—about a rock 'n' roll musician supposedly dead of a heroin overdose who turns up in his old band unrecognized by his own bandmates ("Even when I was alive, they didn't know it was me"), a disappeared billionaire developer, a gang of right-wing thugs called Vigilant California, a criminal empire so vast and invulnerable even to speak its name is to make the earth tremble, the first, primitive, bootlegged version of the Internet, and an old girlfriend—people were already talking about the great hippie detective novel. About a dope deal, of course—and an outsider version of Philip Marlowe or Lew Archer. Roger Simon's Moses Wine—starting out in 1973 with *The Big Fix* and still on the case thirty years later, wasn't it. In 1971 Hunter Thompson played the role well in "Fear and Loathing in Las Vegas," but soon dissolved in his own aura. Pynchon's Doc Sportello somehow realizes the fantasy.

About to turn thirty, he lives in Gordita Beach, halfway between Hermosa Beach and El Segundo, though not on any

real-life map. He thinks of himself as John Garfield; he's the same height. On his wall is a velvet painting he bought on the street: "a Southern California beach that never was—palms, bikini babes, surfboards, the works."

He thought of it as a window to look out of when he couldn't deal with looking out of the traditional glass-type one in the other room. Sometimes in the shadows the view would light up, usually when he was smoking weed, as if the contrast knob of Creation had been messed with just enough to give everything an underglow, a luminous edge, and promise that the night was about to turn epic somehow.

That's as good a description of "L.A. Woman" as any other. It has the textures of ordinary life, and everything about it is slightly off, because the epic is what it's reaching for, but without giving itself away, without makeup, cool clothes, photo shoots, or any other trappings of Hollywood glamour. Robby Krieger's guitar is in the front of the music, thin and loose, intricate and casual, serious and quick as thought. Jim Morrison is in the back of the sound, as if trailing the band on the street, shouting that he's got this song for them, a new-type song for a dime, it'd be perfect, and you can see the Morrison who's singing, a man who in 1970 did look like a bum, a huge and tangled beard, a gut hanging over his belt, his clothes stained. The voice is full of cracks and burrs, and an inspiring, crazy exuberance, a delight in being on the streets, in the sun, at night under neon, *Blade Runner* starring Charles Bukowski instead of Harrison Ford—this bum doesn't shuffle down the street, he runs, stops, twirls, runs back the way he came. Maybe the city doesn't want to see him, but he's in love with the city and that's the story he has to tell. He's not blind. "Motel money, murder madness," he muses to himself; he can see the fear the Manson gang left in the eyes of the people he passes even as they avert their eyes from his, but he's not afraid, and he knows he's not the killer they're afraid of. The whole song is a chase in pieces, the guitarist tracing half circles in the air, the singer dancing in circles around him, the guitarist not seeing him, the singer not caring.

In *Inherent Vice* there are set pieces lifted, as they have to be, from the likes of *The Little Sister* or *The Chill*—the visit to the big mansion, the hero doped up in the locked room. What is new is Pynchon's depiction of the economy of the hippie utopia as altogether heroin-driven, a suspicion that flits around the edges of the first pages of the story and drives the last sixty pages like a train. What's new in the detective-story novel is Sportello himself, a one-time skip tracer who's graduated into the world of the licensed PI, beach-bum division, and Sportello's nemesis, the infinitely manipulative LAPD homicide detective Bigfoot Bjornsen, who could have stepped out of H. P. Lovecraft. "It's like," he says, "there's this evil sub-god who rules over Southern California? who off and on will wake from his slumber and allow the dark forces that are always lying there just out of the sunlight to come forth? . . . bye-bye, Black Dahlia, rest in peace Tom Ince, we've seen the last of those good old-time L.A. murder mysteries I'm afraid. We've found the gateway to hell, and it's asking far too much of your L.A. civilian not to want to go crowding on through it, horny and giggling as always, looking for that latest thrill. Lots of overtime for me and the boys I guess, but it brings us all that much closer to the end of the world"—and you can almost see Squeaky Fromme, not to mention four or five previous generations of Southern California mystics and psychics, perched on his shoulder, smiling like Natalie Wood.

Manson's shadow is everywhere, whether it's Sportello and a black militant arguing over who's hotter, Fromme or Leslie van Houten ("Submissive, brainwashed, horny little teeners," says Sportello's old girlfriend Shasta Hepworth, "who do exactly what you want before you even know what that is . . . Your kind of chick, Doc, that's the lowdown on you"), or Sportello and three other people in a car pulled over for no reason they can see. "New program," says a cop, "you know how it is, another excuse for paperwork, they're calling it Cult-watch, every gathering of three or more civilians is now defined as a potential cult." It's a joke people use because the punch line is all around them, until Manson changes into a story so sensational no one thinks to look behind it, into "a vortex of corroded history," into what Don DeLillo, in *Great Jones Street*, a novel set about the same time as Pynchon's, called "the true underground," where presidents and prime ministers "make the underground deals and speak the true underground idiom," where "the laws are broken, way down under, far beneath the speed freaks and the cutters of smack."

Out of all this, Pynchon can produce a beach joint where customers argue convincingly "about the two different 'Wipeout' singles, and which label, Dot or Decca, featured the laugh and which didn't." He can craft a shootout that turns on a line that in any other hands would be ridiculous, but on Pynchon's ground feels right—a line that to get off the ground needs a whole book behind it, a line that hits the note the book needs to lift itself into the air. "He waited till he saw a dense patch of moving shadow, sighted it in, and fired, rolling away immediately, and the figure dropped like an acid tab into the mouth of Time"—a moment that fades into an ending so delicate and tragic in its apprehension of all that is soon to pass away it could change places with the last page of *Tender Is the Night*.

You can hear the last pages of the story Pynchon tells in "L.A. Woman" as the Doors played it at the end of 1970, in Dallas, on December 11, the day before their last show, in New Orleans. "It also looked like a crime scene waiting on its next crime," Pynchon writes; if you had that image in your head, you might hear it playing out as, from the stage of the State Fair Music Hall, "L.A. Woman" begins. It's spooky, immediately calling down night fog. On the tape that survives, the band sounds very far away. Morrison screams out an enormous *Yeeeaaahhh!* and then there's nothing, only a beat moving without a destination. Even as something like music begins to take shape, all you hear is restraint, a refusal to move—a suspension that would turn a corner the next night, the Doors' last night, when in the midst of his performance Morrison began to slam his microphone down until the boards broke, then sat on the stage and refused to move or sing. Pynchon could have reviewed that show: "It was as if whatever had happened had reached some kind of limit. It was like finding the gateway to the past unguarded, unforbidden because it didn't have to be." Or rewritten it as a dream: "Doc followed the prints of her bare feet already collapsing into rain and shadow, as if in a fool's attempt to find his way back into a past that despite them both had gone on into the future it did."

In Dallas, after almost three minutes, Morrison begins to sing, directly, conversationally, without pressure, with long waits between lines. As anyone will be able to hear months later, when *L.A. Woman* appears in the stores, the bum on the street is present, but not as he will be then; this man is more damaged, his speech slurred, his demeanor distracted, someone screaming at himself, tearing at his clothes.

As the performance takes shape all four of the musicians sound as if they are so sure of the song they can trust it to keep going even if they seem to stop playing it. And they do seem to stop, over and over again, less playing the song than listening to it. The characters in the song—the man singing, the city, the woman the man is chasing in his mind—are specters, figments of each other's imagination. And then, after the bum is replaced by a preacher, who declaims and chants, from a little bit softer now to a little bit louder now, a little bit louder now, until *risin' risin' risin' risin'!* sweeps through the music, a spell is broken. Everything is clear. The bum is just a bum, the city is just streets and freeways, the woman is just the last person the bum saw before he opened his mouth.

Near the end, after more than fourteen minutes, the band, playing the song like a theme, begins to drop away. You can almost see the drummer, the guitarist, and the organ player leave the stage as a stranger walks out of the wings and onto the stage as if he had no intention of being there but is willing to make the best of it. "Well," he says, just like a friend would say if you ran into him on the street, no attitude, no pose, "I just got into town about an hour ago"—what's new?

"L.A. Woman," *L.A. Woman* (Elektra, 1971). The first and only Doors album not produced by Paul Rothchild, who had quit; their new producer, Bruce Botnick, who had engineered their previous albums, gave the band a freedom in the studio, a sense of ordinary life, that they were ready to use.

———, State Fair Music Hall, Dallas, December 11, 1970, from *Boot Yer Butt! The Doors Bootlegs* (Rhino Handmade, 2003).

Thomas Pynchon, *Inherent Vice* (New York: Penguin Press, 2009), 19, 254–55, 86, 6, 209, 304, 179, 101, 327, 83, 351, 314.

Don DeLillo, *Great Jones Street* (Boston: Houghton Mifflin, 1973), 231–32.

Mystery Train

COMING OFF A SEAMLESS seven minutes of "Roadhouse Blues" in Pittsburgh on May 2, 1970—a Corvette shifting through five gears again and again, just to show off how smooth the transmission is—the band paused, and Jim Morrison took a breath. "People get ready," he crooned, holding up the Impressions nightclub brotherhood anthem like a racetrack flag— "People get ready / For that train to glory"—but that wasn't the train the group was about to take out of the station.

For more than three slow minutes, with the guitar counting off the pace of an engine picking up steam with scratchy clickety-clack and the organ moving much faster, trees and rivers and strip malls passing by as you looked out the window, the song grew until Morrison could jump it. He got on at the right time, but the music didn't need him: it was loose, taking its own shape. He sang for a few moments, the rhythm reforming thickly around his gross, slobbery voice, everything slurred, then gave the tune back to the band, then came back, then threw it away again.

The song went on, picking up new titles as it continued through ten, twelve, finally nearly fifteen minutes—"Away in India," "Crossroads Blues"—but it was all one song, all one attempt to get somewhere, to get out, to cross a border. As the music edged into its seventh minute, it seemed to have developed a mind of its own: you can hear the song musing over itself, the wheels feeling the tracks, the engine wondering at the rightness of a machine tied to a road of iron, the machine achieving a lightness, a weightlessness, that makes the tracks disappear.

As soon as Morrison came back, all of that was gone, smeared with florid vowels, shapeless words. Again the band finds its way back to its first rhythm, that scratch, and again Morrison flattens it, throwing bits of blues songs out the window, forgetting them as soon as he does; when you're picking blues lines out of the air, there's never any end to them, they're just used tickets, and worth as much.

In the mid-sixties, when the Doors began, when "Mystery Train" first entered their repertoire, Elvis Presley was a joke. The shocking black leather blues he conjured on national television for his 1968 Christmas special was unimaginable after years of movie travelogues, of hula hoops and shrimp, of a world where a racetrack was just another beach—where, as Elvis himself once put it, he had to beat up guys before he sang to them. But in 1968, when Elvis sang "One Night"— after climbing mountains and fording rivers all across the frontiers of "Tryin' to Get to You," going back again and again to Jimmy Reed's "Baby What You Want Me to Do" as if it were a talisman of a treasure he couldn't name, each time deepening it, dropping words in search of a rhythm the song didn't even know it wanted and now couldn't live without— what returned was the sense of awe, of disbelief, that greeted him when he first made himself known.

In the years before that, his "Mystery Train," recorded in 1955 for Sun Records in Memphis—before, so the story went, the money machines in Hollywood and New York turned him into a sausage—had over time acquired a patina of purity. There was an elegance in the recording that couldn't be denied. With Elvis's direct, frank tone and the spare accompaniment, the performance was a veil of simplicity and elusiveness: how could anything so plain feel so otherworldly? The coolest DJs, the most sophisticated connoisseurs, chose "Mystery Train" as their one transcendent Elvis-object—less, it seemed, to signify the genius a poor country boy had traded for money and renown, but to show that even the dumbest rube could, for a moment, stumble on the sublime.

"Mystery Train" was the bohemian's Elvis: a small, perfectly crafted work of art, with a charge of unlikeliness that took it out of the realm of craft and into the realm of event, something that once present in the world could neither be repeated nor taken back. Those who knew celebrated it like the expatriate Argentine intellectuals and dandies in Julio Cortázar's *Hopscotch* obsessing in Paris over Bix Beiderbecke and Bessie Smith, but there was none of this in Jim Morrison's "Mystery Train." He had his own Elvis obsession—unlike any rock 'n' roll singer since "Heartbreak Hotel" devoured the world's airwaves, he had Elvis's Greek-god looks, his seductive vampire's hooded eyes; like Elvis he communicated the disdain of the beautiful for the ordinary world. But he faced "Mystery Train" as if it were itself an object of disdain: something that had to be wrecked. It was more than a year since the night in Miami that left Morrison facing felony charges for indecent exposure and the Doors banned across the country. Well before that, Morrison had come on stage drunk, sometimes babbling, lashing out, sometimes at the crowd, sometimes at phantoms only he could see; he appeared on stage in a fog of self-loathing, and he could hate the songs he had to sing as deeply and as expansively as he could hate his bandmates, his audience, and himself. As he gropes his way through "Mystery Train," the feeling in the performance is that the song needs someone as close to Elvis Presley as Jim Morrison could imagine himself to be to give the song the lie it always contained: Forget about art. You're a sausage. I'm a sausage. The world is meat.

Against it all, each time Morrison leaves the song to the band the band tries to reclaim it, and each time it does. So once again Morrison lumbers back to spit, to trip, to upend the beat. His disdain—the refusal to credit one kind of beauty, the abstract beauty of art, even as you trade on another kind, the material beauty of the body—was there almost from the start.

On December 10, 1967, Otis Redding's plane went down in a lake in Wisconsin. The greatest soul singer since Sam Cooke, he was only twenty-six, but in the fissures of his voice he seemed much older, someone who had lived more than one life, who had played each part in the moral dramas of "I've Been Loving You Too Long (To Stop Now)," "Pain in My Heart," "These Arms of Mine." In "Try a Little Tenderness," in "I've Got Dreams to Remember," he too had the elegance that comes out of Elvis's "Mystery Train" like perfume—that sense of perfect balance in the midst of music that promises it can go anywhere in any moment. And so it was bizarre, it was hard to believe your ears, when barely two weeks later, at Winterland in San Francisco, Jim Morrison took the stage with the Doors and out over the hall went a few lines recast from Lead Belly's "Poor Howard," but now smug, leering, a Lead Belly song that sounded like a frat-boy chant: "Poor Otis, dead and gone / Left me here to sing his song." As if you could!

Pissing on Redding's grave—it was beyond arrogant, it was beyond obnoxious, it was even beyond racism, or for that matter the racelessness of a white singer embracing a black singer as a brother, if any of that was even there. It was Morrison pantomiming pissing on his own grave—when the time came, he would be barely a year older than Redding was. Who knew: someone could come along one day with "Poor Jim, dead and gone—"

There's an echo of that moment—that prediction—as, after eleven minutes of "Mystery Train" that night in Pittsburgh, Morrison stumbles into "Bullfrog Blues," if that is what he's stumbling into, if instead of the perfect blues lines "Woke up this morning, bullfrogs on my mind" he's singing "Woke up this morning, the girlfriend on my mind"—as if I could tell one from the other, his tone says. "Train I ride, sixteen coaches long / Train I ride, sixteen coaches long," he'd begun, like Elvis, like the blues singer Junior Parker, recording the song he co-wrote two years before Elvis took it up. "Well, that mean old train / Took my baby he gone"—Morrison was already tripping over the song, finding himself in the Golden Chords in 1958, when then–Robert Zimmerman rewrote the song as "Big Black Train": "Well, big black train, coming down the line / Well, big black train, coming down the line / Well, you got my woman, you bring her back to me / Well, that cute little chick is the girl I want to see." As Morrison went on, there was a hint of someone taking a story from the song that the song had never told before: "Train, train, coming down the line / Train, train, coming down the line / Well, that mean old train, took the only friend of mine." Still, it was all too casual, too thrown away to pull anyone else onto the train.

But now he's waking up with bullfrogs on his mind. He translates what that might mean, and he lights up the old phrase, changing its poetry into ordinary language and back again: "Well, I woke up this morning, eight miles on my mind" (or "H-bomb on my mind," or "Nothing on my mind"). He goes back to the prosaic: "I woke up this morning, railroad on my mind." "Take a little walk with me," he says, grabbing on to a floating blues phrase that from song to song can mean love or death and anything in between, a line that is never a promise without a threat, a smile without a warning: "Everything gonna work out fine." He begins to scream the line, the soft, shapeless voice he's had throughout the performance now tearing like cardboard: "Everything, everything, everything gonna work out fine!" He presses even harder, until suddenly emotions are breaking up like a house in a storm, and each one is true: hysteria, fear, happiness at finally getting the music right. The band had pushed itself into a conventional fast, noisy, meaningless, phony frenzy; it could be that this is what allows Morrison to step forward as if what he's singing is something other than meaningless or phony. "Whoa-*whoa!*" he screams, stretching the vowels into the next day, throwing them out ahead of himself like a harpoon. It's a shout of pleasure, doubling back in its own echo, as if, as you listen, it's gone past death around the bend and back again—and just like that, the band is coming up deliberately behind him, that clean clickety-clack is again driving the music, even as the pace slows, crawls, as finally the train is pulling into the station. In Junior Parker's version, as a friend once said, at the end you can actually hear the air brakes; here you can feel the train go right up to the railhead and stop. "People get ready," Morrison says again—the corny device of ending a story with the same words with which you began it saying that this was just a show, but something else is there, too.

There is a genie the group can let loose that can, at any time, leave you with the sense that you have made a journey, that you have been somewhere you haven't been before, that you have not altogether returned to where you began, perhaps because you didn't want to, because the allure of what you've seen is too strong to altogether surrender. And accompanying that sense of movement is grandeur, a sense that the story you've been told is bigger than life. All through its quarter-hour, its pieces and fragments, through the singer's fatuous refusal to acknowledge the shapeliness of the song he is, in his own way, refusing to sing, you can hear that this is what the Doors were chasing; you can hear them catch it, and you can hear them let it go.

"Mystery Train," Pittsburgh City Arena, May 2, 1970, *Live in Pittsburgh 1970* (DMC/Bright Midnight/Rhino, 2008). As performed in Honolulu the month before, on April 18, 1970, the song is less shapely, but for long stretches—the organ-driven middle break, Morrison digging into the wind in the word "India," the final "Woke up this morning" refrains—more explosive, the band finding itself, as an idea, a mission, a sound that remained to be tracked down, as they caught a ride on their own music. See *Boot Yer Butt! The Doors Bootlegs* (Rhino Handmade, 2003). The audience tape runs out at 13.48, clearly well before the performance ended.

Elvis Presley, "Mystery Train" (Sun, 1955).

Little Junior's Blue Flames, "Mystery Train" (Sun, 1953).

The End, 1966

Early on, Robby Krieger developed a way of saying, in a very few, quiet, spaced notes on his guitar, that something was about to happen. He could make you draw your breath.

It happened first with "The End," the closing track of *The Doors*, released in January 1967, recorded in August the year before, not long after the notorious debut of the song at the Whisky à Go Go on Sunset Strip. In the studio the song unwinds over nearly twelve minutes; those first notes tell you to suspend any expectations of how long this is going to last. A tambourine shivers off to the side of the sound, like something out of Robert Johnson's "Come on in My Kitchen"—a rattlesnake version of Johnson's whispered "Can't you hear the wind blow?" when he brings that perfect recording almost to a halt.

"Specialize in having fun!" Jim Morrison sang in the song before, "Take It as It Comes"; the words didn't match the music. The band was both light on its feet and relentless, and what was coming, what you were going to have to take, felt dark, hard, irresistible, a test, not anything you could expect.

"The End" was the test. Two minutes in, Krieger plays an atonal figure against a steady count, Ray Manzarek shifts quietly behind him, a green river in the cave of the song, and—a minute, a minute and a half has passed, but there's no sense of time passing—John Densmore hits his drums off the beat, louder each time, fracturing the sound, until you can see his kit tumbling like Keith Moon's, the sound so big you can see an avalanche of drums burying everyone else.

This is a repeating moment; events like this occur across the span of "The End." All through the piece, there will be incidents when the performance feels as if it's about to tear itself to pieces. It's a question of rhythm. The furious, impossibly sustained assault that will steer the song to its end, a syncopation that swirls on its own momentum, each musician called upon not just to match the pace of the others but to draw his own pictures inside the maelstrom—in its way this is a relief, because that syncopation gives the music a grounding you can count on, that you can count off yourself.

There were exciting pauses in "Take It as It Comes," when the band pulled back from itself, letting the song loose, letting it tell them where to take it next. Instruments dropped out, but a pulse always held: it was better than most of what was on the radio, but not a new language, a foreign language you had to learn. In "The End" the pauses were traffic accidents, what in the 1920s the Berlin dadaist Richard Huelsenbeck called "the art of yesterday's crash." Throughout the song, until that final surge, everything seems tentative, uncertain, unclear; that's the source of the song's power, its all-encompassing embrace of darkness, gloom, and dread, and it's this insistence on the uncertain, on working without a ground, that takes the performance past its own corniness. Morrison's words have the feel of phrases made up on the spot to fit or break the rhythms taking shape around him: the languid, sleepy "The west, is the best" followed by the staccato jump in the way the last five words of "Get here—and we'll do the rest" pull the first two words after them like a weight pulling a house off a cliff. There is the drifting chase after a blue bus, a chase that is a matter of someone walking slowly, deliberately, no matter how fast the bus is going, knowing that sooner or later he'll catch it and climb on.

Morrison's voice in the slides in the music that seem to matter most—at the beginning and the end, where "my only friend" is brought into the song and then banished, so the singer can contemplate the perfection of his own isolation, his own renunciations, his own beauty—is full, creamy, a deep well. You could drop a coin into the pool of this voice and never hear the splash. As the voice opens over words or syllables—"friend," "only," "die"—the words change shape, gliding out into the empty spaces in the sound. In the way Morrison raises the "end" in the first "This is the end" up past the words preceding it, as if to make sure you don't miss its significance, carries the smell of falsity, pretention, bad poetry; the plain flatness of "my only friend" instantly takes *the end* down to a plane of ordinary life, lets the listener into the song, and sets the words free to find their traveling companions. No element in the music seems to anticipate any other, to call any other forth; the performance is a dance around a fire, with the pace determined by the flickers, which can't be anticipated, that are never the same—not until the set piece in the center, when the singer says he wants to kill his father and fuck his mother.* The suggestion of the singer reenacting the murder of the Clutter family, but from inside the family, the truly suggestive moment of this part of the song, is erased by the cheapness of shoving Oedipus into the drama: the singer goes quietly into his sister's room, then into his brother's room, he could leave them both dead, he could just be making sure they're asleep, but when he gets to his father and his mother— when he gets to what one friend calls "the 'Hello Faddah, hello Muddah' extravaganza"—you realize you've heard this story before. That gorgeous tone for single words that make a drama so much richer than this one here changes the white marble of Michelangelo's *David* to the plaster of the statuettes you can buy in the gift shop.

Minutes later, with the music gathering itself for its final charge, the real drama takes place. Krieger, Manzarek, and Densmore are pushing for a centrifugal momentum that will create its own Big Bang, until each piece flies away from the other; Morrison, his one-legged, spread-eagled stage dance now playing out on his tongue, is the controlling rhythmic force. "Fuck, fuck, fuck, fuck," he snaps, snarls, talking into a mirror, testing the word for its feel in his mouth, finding the same brittle, syncopated click with which Krieger opened the theme, the word *fuck* buried but viscerally changing shape

---

*Morrison refused to change "higher" in "Light My Fire" for *The Ed Sullivan Show*, but in "The End" for the recording studio he substituted a strangled "Arrragghhh" for the "Fuck you"—or "Fuck you all night long"—he used on stage.

each time he spits it out, the word cutting itself short, *fuk*, distorting, *fut*, cracking, *fak*, curling around itself, *fug*.

Everything slows down again, and the song returns to the beckoning, the foreshadowing, of its first moments. Wherever it was you started from, you have traveled somewhere else, and no time at all has passed. As the Firesign Theatre had their professor say when he entered his time machine, "I will be gone for a thousand years, but to you it will seem only like a moment."

"The End," *The Doors* (Elektra, 1967).

Firesign Theatre, "The Further Adventures of Nick Danger," from *How Can You Be in Two Places at Once When You're Not Anywhere at All?* (Columbia, 1969). The group's *Everything You Know Is Wrong* (Columbia, 1974) includes a groaning old-Indian parody of the snake section of "The End."

The Doors in the So-called Sixties

FOR THREE YEARS, visiting my father in the nursing home where he lived, I would drive across the Bay Bridge from Berkeley to San Francisco and back again, twenty or twenty-five minutes over, twenty or twenty-five minutes back. In the spring of 2010 I made an interesting discovery: in those forty or fifty minutes, switching stations to find something I wanted to hear, cutting from 98.5 to 104.5 to 103.7 to 107.7 to 90.7 as soon as a song I liked was over, sometimes catching signals floating in and out, half a tune before it broke up or was drowned out by something else, I was all but guaranteed to hear all or part of Lady Gaga's "Bad Romance" at least three times, and Train's "Hey, Soul Sister" at least twice. This was not a sur- prise; those were the big hits of the season, and both were wonderful—bottomless, each in its own way. With "Hey, Soul Sister," there was the delirium of the guy dancing in his bedroom as he watched his favorite video on his computer screen, over and over just as people all over the world were now listening to him. The song changed in its emotional meter from one nonsense verse to the next, from the impassioned chorus to the way a banjo isolated the singer in his little drama, the way the band crashing down on the same phrase a stanza later brought him into a greater drama, just one of a million people dreaming the same dream. With "Bad Romance" there was first the delirium of the production, what seemed like thousands of little pieces all spun by some all-seeing, thousand-eared overmind into a Busby Berkeley chorus line of sounds instead of legs. There was the cruelty of the singer, mocking whoever the *you* in the song was, sneering, turning her back, looking back over her shoulder with a look that killed, shouting at him or her on the street so everyone can hear: "'Cause I'm a freak, *baby*"—the last word squeezed in the sound, the *b* and the *y* cut off just slightly at the beginning and then at the end, so that it's less a word than a spew of pure disgust. And then, with about a minute left on the record, everything changes. "I don't wanna be friends": a desperation invades the performance, trivializes, erases, everything that's come before it, and pushes on, a completely different person now telling a completely different story, tearing at her hair, her clothes, scratching out her own eyes, then with her dada chant cutting it all off like someone breaking through the last frame of a film to shout "THE END!" I loved them both; I got lost in them each time.

In a way, each record contained its own surprise every time it came on—but the real surprise was something else. As certain as it was that I'd hear "Bad Romance" "Bad Romance"

"Hey, Soul Sister" "Bad Romance" "Hey Soul Sister," it was close to a sure thing that I'd hear the Doors twice, three times, even four times—and not just "Light My Fire." Not just the one or two songs into which the radio has compressed Bob Dylan ("Like a Rolling Stone"), the Rolling Stones ("Gimmie Shelter," maybe "(I Can't Get No) Satisfaction," entered in the log of time as just "Satisfaction" to save conceptual space), the Byrds ("Mr. Tambourine Man"), Wilson Pickett ("In the Midnight Hour"), Sly and the Family Stone ("Everyday People), the Band ("The Weight"), all of the Doors contemporaries save the Beatles, as if they were forgotten hacks forever playing the same squalid dive with the same announcement on the door, the name of the one hit maybe bigger than the name of the act because you can always remember the song even if you can't remember who did it, even if whoever is doing it now isn't exactly whoever did it then:

Creedence Clearwater Revisited
("PROUD MARY")
Thunder Valley Casino • Resort

—with, turning just two pages in the newspaper entertainment listings on May 5, 2011—

John Fogerty
("PROUD MARY")
Cache Creek Casino Resort*

---

*Or for that matter the Doors themselves—when in 2003 Ray Manzarek and Robby Krieger reformed the band under its own name with Ian Astbury of the Cult hanging on to the microphone stand, 1960s video footage and a pyschedelic light show projected behind them, and Ty Dennis, late of the terrible L.A. new wave band the Motels, substituting for John Densmore, who refused to take part.

At any given moment in 2010 you could hear "Light My Fire," "People Are Strange," "Moonlight Drive," "Touch Me," "Love Her Madly," "L.A. Woman," "Twentieth Century Fox," "Riders on the Storm," "Hello, I Love You," "Five to One," "Break on Through (To the Other Side)," "Soul Kitchen," "Roadhouse Blues." What were all these songs doing there? And why did most of them sound so good?

As I reveled in the music, as if I hadn't heard it before— realizing, in some sense, that I hadn't: that "L.A. Woman" and "Roadhouse Blues" had never sounded so big, so unsatisfied, so free in 1970 and 1971 as they did forty years later—I remembered Oliver Stone's 1991 movie *The Doors*. The reviews were terrible: "What a shame to have to take your clothes off for a movie like this," one critic wrote at the time of Meg Ryan's nude scene. I'd expected to hate the film, to watch shows I'd seen and music I'd loved faked and frozen; instead I was shocked at how right it felt, how even the most overplayed scenes still seemed to leave something out: smugness, easy answers, a director's superiority to his own material. The picture was alive; I could replay the movie just by thinking about it.

It came out a year after *Pump Up the Volume*, Allan Moyle's film about a teenager's clandestine radio station in a faceless Arizona suburb. I couldn't get either one out of my head. I didn't want to. But when I tried to tell people about the movies, about why they ought to see them, and, usually, failed to convince them that they should, I realized both films were trapped in the same prison: the prison of the Sixties, not as a period in which people actually lived, but as an idea, or the scrim of an idea, meant to keep all lived experience, all unanswered, unasked questions, as far away as possible. I began to think about why these Sixties—as opposed to a lowercased sixties, or whatever years one might choose to apply to the period (1958–69, from the Beats to Altamont, some have said; 1963–74, from John F. Kennedy's assassination to Richard Nixon's resignation; 1964–68, from the Beatles to the assassinations of Bobby Kennedy and Martin Luther King)— hadn't gone away, and why, perhaps, they never would.

A few years before, in the late 1980s, when I found myself constantly getting calls about the Sixties from newspaper and TV reporters, I decided I wasn't going to talk about it anymore. There was a flood of ludicrous media-created anniversaries: the twenty-fifth anniversary of the Beatles' first appearance on *The Ed Sullivan Show*, the twentieth anniversary of Woodstock, the twentieth anniversary of the Rolling Stones' deadly free concert at Altamont—as if, on the twentieth anniversary of the day Hell's Angels stabbed and beat a young man named Meredith Hunter to death as the Rolling Stones played "Under My Thumb," people who'd been there, or people who might as well have been there, who'd somehow been convinced that the event was a symbolic turning point in their lives and culture, would turn to each other and say, "Wow! Next Tuesday's going to be the twentieth anniversary of Altamont! Let's all get dressed up like Hell's Angels and naked acid casualties and have a party!" 2007 was if anything worse: forty is traditionally a meaningless year for anniversaries, but the media looked at the calendar and just like that 1967 was, until the page turned, the most important year in history. You weren't *there*? every TV, magazine cover, radio station seemed to ask, or rather taunt. You don't remember the day the Beatles' *Sgt. Pepper* came out? The Six-Day War? The Monterey Pop Festival? The Summer of Love? The first Doors album?

"What is the meaning of Beatles Woodstock Altamont *today?*" people would ask me on the phone twenty years before that. "There's *no* meaning," I would say, irritated, but also confused. "Why are you doing this story?" I'd ask them. They didn't know; they weren't in charge. They were just told to go out and get the story, and someone said I might know, as if I, or anyone my age, might have some secret we were keeping.

The implication seemed to be that anyone who might know had nothing better to do than to sit around wondering about the meaning of events that, at the time, had mostly felt like fun, or not fun. As if one's life had been empty ever since. That, I realized, was the secret behind the media's need for these stories, or non-stories. The media had a sense that ever since the 1960s, life had been empty. That nothing had happened since: nothing worth memorializing, anyway. And that too was part of the media secret, the idea of memorializing. The anniversaries were attempted funerals. They were attempts to bury something. But the funeral never seemed to end, and the burial never seemed complete.

I thought of a *New Yorker* cartoon: a nicely dressed middle-aged woman stands in her nice living room and turns to her husband, who's got a big paunch, who's draped in a chair looking miserable, exhausted, unkempt. "Honey," she says, "the '60s are over." This would have been funny in 1980, when Ronald Reagan was first elected president. The cartoon appeared in 1988, just before Ronald Reagan left the White House. And that was all too right. Ronald Reagan was a Sixties person if anyone was; the negation of the mythic Sixties, but Sixties nonetheless. "In his early years Elvis Presley was virtually apolitical," the columnist and novelist Michael Ventura wrote in 1987. "Yet no one else in the '50s except Martin

Luther King had as huge a political effect in the United States. Elvis single-handedly created what came to be known as the youth market, the demand for the form of music he made popular. Through being united as a market, that particular wave of youth felt the cohesion of community that became the '60s upheaval, an upheaval that all our politics since have been in reaction to, for, or against."

Like Newt Gingrich dismissing Bill and Hillary Clinton as "counter-culture McGoverniks," by which he meant beatniks, by which he meant *Sputnik,* by which he meant commies, it was by setting himself so firmly and grandly against that upheaval that Ronald Reagan became a national figure. In 1966, running for governor in California, he ran against the Berkeley Free Speech Movement of two years before, and won; in 1980 he ran against the Sixties as such, just as Margaret Thatcher had done in the U.K. the year before. Both did better than simply run against the Sixties: they kept the time and the idea alive by co-opting its rhetoric, by so brilliantly taking its watchwords, or its slogans, as their own. "Adventure," "risk," "a new world"—those were emblems no conservative movements had claimed since the 1930s, when the movements that did trumpet such words named themselves fascist. Unlike their formal political ancestors—Republican presidents Warren Harding, Calvin Coolidge, Herbert Hoover, Dwight D. Eisenhower, Nixon, or Conservative prime ministers Winston Churchill or Anthony Eden—Reagan and Thatcher were utopians. They were impossible and unthinkable without the Sixties, and the 1960s, without the idea and the years actually lived. They couldn't afford to let them die.

Around the time *The Doors* appeared in theaters, a nineteen-year-old friend came to ask me for help with a college paper he was writing on the 1960s. Here was someone I'd known all his life, and in 1991 he wanted to talk about the Haight-Ashbury in San Francisco in 1967, about the Grateful Dead—not because this was ancient history, but because it wasn't. He knew too many Deadheads his own age. He was trying to understand what all this had to do with him: why were his friends dressing up like their parents had or hadn't twenty-five years before and going to the same shows? I tried to tell him how strange that seemed to me, how impossible it would have been for me and my friends to have put on suits in 1965 and call ourselves Benny Goodmanheads or even Billie Holidayheads. But I couldn't get that across. I wanted to tell him about *Pump Up the Volume*, about hints of something new coming out of a cultural desert, but that too seemed out of reach.

As I'd watched my own daughters grow up—in 1991 the oldest was twenty-one, born just days after Altamont; my wife stayed home, because we figured if the baby was born there we'd have to name it Mick, and because we had heard Hell's Angels would be there and we knew who they were—I followed the growth of this remarkable persistence of a vanished time. I followed it as a form of oppression. It seemed to me that if my own children were to have a chance to make a culture of their own, to make their own history, then the Sixties would have to take their rightful place in the filing cabinet of yesterdays and once-upon-a-times. But all their lives, people who were in their teens and twenties when the Doors, twenty years gone, reappeared as *The Doors* had been told by movies and books and television and the radio that *then* was when it all happened, that *there* were the touchstones of whatever dribs and drabs of art and politics they might flatter themselves to call their own. Over and over, people a generation younger than I am have been told that the sound of which they can claim only the echo happened once, and it won't happen again. When, in 1991, people turned on the radio, or when people turn it on today, and hear Buffalo Springfield's 1966 "For What It's Worth," the record itself or a commercial based on it,* when they hear a tune sparked by riots on Sunset Strip in 1965, with the lines "There's something happening here, what it is ain't exactly clear," one thing *is* clear: you're supposed to feel that something happened, but it isn't happening anymore. You were born at the wrong time; you missed it. "One of my first sentient thoughts as a rock critic," Gina Arnold, one of the best ones, wrote in 1991, "was how incredibly sad it was that I had been born to be a teen in the '70s— too late to have seen the Rolling Stones in their heyday. My first glimpse, in 1976, seemed so late for the train—little did I know they'd drag on for another fifteen years." Would she have believed she could have written the same sentence twenty years later?

Looking at the Berlin Wall falling in 1989, Francis Fukuyama wrote his famous essay–cum–*New Yorker* cartoon "The End of History," announcing that no longer would humanity be troubled by possibilities of change outside of fashion; to his children he bequeathed a life of peace, quiet, and acceptance. Neil Young, a member of Buffalo Springfield when they made "For What It's Worth," watched the same event and recorded a song called "Rockin' in the Free World." He already had a

---

*The Miller Beer version omitted the line "There's a man with a gun over there, telling you you've got to beware," bumping the chorus forward to cover the gap.

long road of oddness behind him. Depending on when you looked, he was addled, confused, quaint, and again and again, someone you hadn't heard before. He'd pretended to be an Indian; he'd said positive, mysterious things about Charles Manson. He wrote and sang "Ohio," a song about the shooting of students at Kent State in 1970 as thrilling as it was bitter; endorsing Reagan in 1984, he'd said, "You can't always support the weak. You've got to make the weak stand up on one leg, half a leg, whatever they've got." "Rockin' in the Free World" was a statement he apparently felt was so crucial he recorded and released it twice, acoustic and electric, live and in the studio, in order to say that the free world was turning its back on freedom.

In the 1989 acoustic version, the audience is as present in the sound as the singer, violently ignoring the singer's every violent denunciation of what his country has come to. As Young sings about a dead crack baby "who'll never go to school, never get to fall in love, never get to be cool"—if those lines aren't rock 'n' roll, what is?—the people in the crowd cheer, yell, stomp, raise fists, pump arms in the air: Free World! Alright! We won! They're so excited that this Sixties person is right there, in the flesh: they can tell someone they saw him before he died. The audience sounds as if it's tossing a beach ball back and forth as the guy on stage sings about the death of all he holds dear.

It feels terrible; it feels fine. The sound from the stage and the sound from the crowd say that for one interesting public person, nothing has been settled. That he's standing in front of a big crowd playing an acoustic guitar to sing his song for people who are oblivious to what he has to say suggests that someday he might be standing on a corner with a guitar case open at his feet. It's a promise that he'll always shout, even if his shout won't be heard, a promise that an unheard shout is its own power principle, precisely because in the world of pop culture what isn't heard doesn't exist. That shout is the tree falling unheard and thus the tree that never fell, until, years later, the echo shakes the world like an earthquake. Young acts out this paradox: he performs as a Sixties relic who is not a relic, whose best music is at once behind him and yet to be made. He insists it is still his place to describe history, to name it a betrayal and declare himself unsatisfied.

That is Oliver Stone with *The Doors*. Stone was in his midforties when he made the picture. Behind him were *Salvador*, *Platoon*, *Wall Street*, *Talk Radio*, *Born on the Fourth of July*, all of them overstated, overplayed, overdone, powerful. He was a man obsessed with his place in history, and obsessed with proving to himself and to the world that he was part of it. He enlisted in the Army to fight in Vietnam because he was afraid he might miss it—that he might, in words the critic Leslie Fiedler wrote about the 1930s, miss "the mythic life of his generation."* For Stone the past is present. He wasn't there to see what the Doors did back in the 1960s, when they, his movie says, acted out the mythic life of their generation; he heard their music twisted by history, heard it on Armed Forces Radio

---

*Unless, as Eve Babitz, much closer to Jim Morrison than most who would claim to be, put it at the time Stone's movie was released, "Oliver Stone was so uncool he voluntarily went to Vietnam instead of prowling around the Sunset Strip with the rest of his generation. Oliver Stone was such a nerd he became a soldier, a Real Man. He didn't understand that in the '60s real men were not soldiers. A real man was Mick Jagger in *Performance*, in bed with two women, wearing eye makeup and kimonos." In *The Doors*, Stone played Morrison's UCLA film professor, tough but fair.

and on bootleg tapes in Vietnam. The film is a denial that he missed it, a denial so loud it says one thing: I didn't miss it, but you did.

That was the feeling in the ad campaign, with terribly hokey lines cut into radio spots over background Doors music: first the somber "The ceremony is about to begin," then the call to action, "We've gotta make the myths!" That was the feeling in the interviews Stone gave to promote the film. "What does this movie have to say to a '90s audience?" he asked himself in one, and he answered himself: "Freedom. Now. It once existed . . . But there's a religious fundamentalism returning to this country. And people like me are going to be bonfires." It was a heroic act to make this movie, he wanted you to understand; he was willing to be martyred for it. Six dollars and you could watch. The movie should have been awful. Instead it was terrifying.

My wife and I stood in line with scores of people in their teens and twenties. We felt cast out of time, waiting with people who seemingly wanted to claim as more theirs than ours what we'd once gone to see every weekend. I wondered why they had no culture of their own to rebuke us with. I felt the Sixties I hate: something unnamable, like the last unkillable remnants of a disease, a virus with no antidote, a disease of "Freedom . . . It once existed." A disease of freedom *then*, cursing new generations not with their own St. Vitus's Dance, some horrible new upheaval, but with a kind of cultural apathy, a sleeping sickness. What does it mean to pay to watch other people be free? What does it mean to pay to watch dead people be free? "All the *National Lampoon* parodies of the alternative culture have come true," Elvis Costello said in an interview published the same month *The Doors* was released.

"Now you really can get '60s *Golden Protest Favorites,* a historical view which completely distorts that time. When you were 15 or 16 it was an enormously exciting time, and reading the magazines then you were really believing the sense that there was gonna be a revolution in '68, and then this moment of it 'not happening.' Now there's the 'approved' version, which is that it was some kind of nice outing people went through and then didn't so much wise up as start feeling sorry for themselves during the Carter administration, and then got embittered and self-serving during the Reagan administration. These historical vandals are changing history, putting spin control on it even before it's finished." Reading the reviews, you couldn't have expected anything different from Oliver Stone.

All I remembered of the Doors—all I remembered from the hundreds of times I played their first album, from the few times I played the ones after that, from the dozen times I saw them on stage—was the complex and twisting thrill of being taken out of myself. It was a sensation captured by Ian McEwan in *The Innocent,* a novel that ends with the fall of the Berlin Wall, in lines about what a young man felt in Berlin more than thirty years before, when he first heard "Heartbreak Hotel," when the song "spoke only of loneliness and despair. Its melody was all stealth, its gloom comically overstated . . . The song's self-pity should have been hilarious. Instead it made Leonard feel worldly, tragic, bigger somehow."

This isn't simply shown in Oliver Stone's movie; it isn't merely recorded, memorialized, wrapped up and presented to you in a neat package with a greeting card reading "Freedom . . . It once existed . . . Wish you'd been here." It isn't presented. It happens.

It happens in a nightclub when the Doors' music is still inches away from them; it happens in concert sequences when Jim Morrison is a star whose best music is seemingly behind him, has been fixed—when, like the movie that exists in its ads rather than on the screen, the Doors were little more than an outfit selling a myth of freedom that already imprisoned them, imprisoned them as a pop group whose only recognized, concrete social role was to get one more hit.

Imagine what it must have been like to make "The End." No matter how comically overstated it sounded then or sounds now, you can hear that it made the people who made it feel free as they made it—worldly, tragic, bigger somehow. You can hear that it let them apprehend the terror of freedom and made them move forward nevertheless, a note at a time. "It was almost a shock when the song was over," the late Paul Rothchild, the Doors' producer, told the pioneering rock critic Paul Williams just after the Doors' first album was released. "I felt emotionally washed. There were four other people in the control room at the time, when the take was over and we realized the tape was still going." Try to imagine the same people in the same studio a year or two later, making "Touch Me," number one in 1968, or "Hello, I Love You," #3 in 1969, songs the Monkees might have blanched at. Hits keep the halls full, but people are there for the instant myth, to see someone else be free, onstage, in front of them. What does it mean for the people in the crowd, or for the people they've paid to watch? "People pay to see others believe in themselves," the Sonic Youth bassist Kim Gordon wrote in 1983. "Maybe people don't know whether they can experience the erotic or whether it exists only in commercials; but on stage, in the midst of rock 'n' roll, many things happen and anything

can happen, whether people come as voyeurs or come to sub-
mit to the moment. As a performer you sacrifice yourself, you
go through the motions and emotions of sexuality for all the
people who pay to see it, to believe that it exists."

In Oliver Stone's movie, and in real life, the Doors made
the myths and were instantly their victims—as people were
more than twenty years later, standing in line to watch it happen. Already in 1968 the Doors were performing not freedom
but its disappearance. This is what is terrifying: the notion that
the Sixties was no grand, simple, romantic time to sell others
as a nice place to visit, but a place, even as it is created, people
know they can never really inhabit, and never escape.

It can seem as if the movie was made solely to give reality,
not meaning, to a few moments when this trap is sprung. The
Sixties—as clothes, drugs, sex, style, politics, art—come forth

as a time and place where people live by breaking rules they know are right, mainly to see what might happen. The Sixties are an arena. Jim Morrison, a confused guy, enters this arena because it's where the action is, and he becomes a new person, someone he doesn't recognize. A few years later, on stage, he performs as a double: the old person watching the new one, just like any fan in the crowd. When the new person looks at the crowd, the crowd that long ago learned just what it wanted from him, no more and no less, a song from a few years before—was it only two years, even last year?—plays in his head: "Now people just get uglier, and I have no sense of time."

In *The Doors*, in a long, delicate dramatization of the first full performance of "The End" at the Whisky à Go Go in 1966, you see the new person, and, in the audience, new people struggling to emerge from the people they were or are. On stage, the band is moving slowly through the first movements of the song: Kyle MacLachlan as Ray Manzarek, Frank Whaley as Robby Krieger, Kevin Dillon as John Densmore, all of them right, and Val Kilmer as Morrison, more than right.

He has more to play with, and he has a subtle touch. In his first role, in *Top Secret!*,* as orange-haired pretty boy secret agent Nick Rivers, Kilmer is being slammed in the face by uniformed Communist thugs. As he loses consciousness, he sees himself running through a high school corridor. He stops another student. "Do you know which room the final chemistry exam is in?" he says. "All the exams are over," says the other

---

*"Hybrid of an Elvis movie and a World War II underground resistance film," in the words of one movie guide, but mainly the 1984 follow-up to the huge Abrahams-Zucker-Zucker comedy *Airplane!*

student robotically. "Haven't you been to class?" "No—" "But it's the end of the semester," says the Twilight Zone kid, losing interest. Kilmer's face is all terror. "No," he says. "No. I haven't studied. I can't believe I'm back in school . . ." As he wakes up, back in the torture chamber, he finds himself strung up from the ceiling. He's being whipped by two goons, and a smile spreads over his face like water: "Thank God," he says.

A scene like that requires that the actor hold something back in each moment. As an actor, he has to stay a step behind the audience; as a character who hasn't read the script, he has to stay a step behind himself. Onstage at the Whisky, Kilmer waits behind his words as he sings them; he'll follow them, one step at a time, but what Kilmer gets across as he sings is that he doesn't know where the words are leading him, and doesn't care. There's no sense at all that the pace is ever going to break; the tension comes from a conflict between the feeling that nothing is happening and the sense that at any moment anything can.

The camera pans through the crowd, its eye behind a red filter. At tables on the main floor, you see well-groomed, well-dressed men and women sitting quietly. As the camera moves up to the balcony against the stop-time of the drums, the vamping sound of the organ, a sound that in 1967 the band will share with the Velvet Underground's "Heroin," women, including Meg Ryan, playing Jim Morrison's girlfriend Pamela Courson, bob their heads up and down, as if trying to will themselves into a trance, or anyway into the song, which is hanging back, moving not toward them but away. A man stands alone at a railing, smoking, looking down. Go-go dancers sway in elevated cages. At the foot of the stage, women of different ages, again all of them well dressed, ogle the singer. But the mood changes as the band refuses to let the music build in any conventional manner, refuses to even hint at a change, a break, a release. Everywhere in the room there is a sense of anticipation and dread. People know what roles they are expected to play, that they have come to the club in order to play—the amused scene-maker, the would-be groupie, the hipster, the fan, the skeptic, the music-business insider—but those roles are beginning to break down.

Everyone means to leave the place talking about what they've seen, ranking it above or below what they saw the night before, but no one expects to leave wanting something different than he or she wanted when they came in. Behind the band, the camera catches the go-go dancers as they stop dancing and turn to watch. Behind the women at the front of the stage, standing, are men and women dressed roughly, their hair straggly. Behind them, against the wall, people are talking, as if to deflect the music coming from the stage. The women at the front are still moving, but the sexual charge that covered their faces a few minutes before has evaporated. The camera fixes on single faces in the crowd, isolating them, and there's a coldness in the faces, as if they're watching a snuff movie: as if they know they aren't going to like what comes next, but can't turn away.

In this long sequence, nothing is stressed, nothing is glamorized. But two performance scenes in the movie as memorable—scenes as carefully thought through, as carefully made—are crude, overblown, too much, and they are if anything more compelling. That's what Oliver Stone is all about as a director; he's a sensitive thug or he's nothing.

The first is the fire concert. The band is playing in the open air on a stage with Greek-like columns. There's a backdrop of flames licking up, too bright to be a light show. Off to the side there's a huge bonfire; naked people dance around it. As Kilmer sings, he sees a small, plain, seductive woman at the side of the stage; she glances at him, he glances at her, back and forth as the music goes on, and when Kilmer looks up again her clothes are gone, as if by pagan magic. It's a displacing moment: Kilmer glimpses that the forces he has unleashed are simply mouths, a maw without a brain; it wants to eat, it doesn't care what.

The scene was shot at a water temple south of San Francisco: a beautiful, ghostly spot on a long, straight, unlit two-lane mountain road. High school kids went there to drink beer, sing songs, to see if our cars could hit a hundred, six car radios tuned to the same station in the parking lot. There never was a Doors concert there, but what Oliver Stone staged was the concert both the place and the band always wanted. It offers a sense of what the Doors' music contained, and what they had to pull back from with "Touch Me" and "Hello, I Love You": annihilation.

This is a sequence that trumpets noise; the second points from noise to silence. The setting is the Dinner Key Auditorium in Miami in 1969, the show that all but ended the band's career, when in self-hatred and hatred of his audience, Morrison tried to think of some final rule to break, some final humiliation, and so, more like a confused little boy than a dirty old man in a public park, exposed himself. The silence Stone got contains the noise that Dave DiMartino, in 1969 a teenager in the Dinner Key crowd, writing twelve years after the fact, describes best: "Phrases remain. Morrison screaming 'THERE ARE NO RULES!' and exhorting those in the 'cheap seats' to rush the stage; after a lengthy pause, the band breaking into 'Touch Me,' which Morrison sang maybe three lines of before screaming 'STOP!' and telling us that the song sucked and that Robbie Krieger wrote it . . . But what I remember above all was the feeling that anything could have happened that night, that Jim Morrison could have died when he dived into the audience at the show's end, that the people in the cheap seats could have trampled those in the more expensive ones and made the Who-in-Cincinnati no big deal years later. The show might have gone on forever, the rest of the band could have quit, right there, onstage. If Morrison had passed out, we might have cheered—part spectators in the Roman colosseum Morrison imagined himself in, part voyeurs, excited and gleeful at the man exposing more of himself than what was in his pants. We simply watched, most of us, and felt the man doing the things we'd like to do and saying the things we always wanted to say."

Oliver Stone puts this on the screen. And then, in the midst of the chaos—with fans leaping naked or clothed on the stage and the stage still seemingly containing more police than fans, the band playing on as if a fight has broken out in the crowd rather than at their feet, then stopping, Kilmer going to pieces but still convincing you his Morrison is saying exactly what he means, the noise and fear and darkness and spotlights making a fire far uglier than anything in the fireworks at the water temple—everything stops. The show goes on, the band plays, the crowd leaps and screams, but there is nothing to hear. It's a moment of complete suspension; Jim Morrison's first, public death. No one else can see it, no one else on the stage or in the audience can hear the absence of all sound hammering in Val Kilmer's rough, bearded face. Anything could have happened, DiMartino wrote, including this: a conjuring, an arrival, of nothing, the show as a vortex that sucked everything into it until there was nothing left behind, a rapture to the void. This is as far as it can go, the movie says, with Kilmer feeling his way through this utopia, this nowhere, in the silence—art, politics, life, death, wish, fear, desire, love and hate. The moment hits not like some defining event in one person's tawdry, finally insignificant life, but as a moment in history.

You could have walked out of Oliver Stone's movie—easy enough to break down, to write off, to write up the next day as junk—with a great echo pounding in your head, an echo you couldn't decipher, an echo with no meaning, only force. It's a good metaphor for a 1960s that in 1991 had no part in the media's Sixties life-support system, that had nothing to do with teenage Deadheads going to see the Grateful Dead. If, as the bumper stickers said then, THERE IS NOTHING LIKE A GRATE- FUL DEAD CONCERT, this isn't what it wasn't like. The echo of that suspended moment is an enormous, thudding silence, the bang the world doesn't end with, and that was, for some, precisely what the world felt like after the show ended, the show of the concert, the show of the times.

It's this silence, this almost physical sense of an absence, that as culture the Sixties bequeathed to the next decades: with all of its stupidities, mysticisms, solipsisms, self-promotions and cons, the sense of a different world. It's a silence that ultimately silences all the endlessly programmed Sixties hits, that mocks their flash. And it's this silence in which *Pump Up the Volume* begins.

A night shot travels over a suburban development. It's 1990, but it could be twenty years later, or forty years earlier: the setting is straight from any number of 1950s or '60s movies about the Trouble in Suburbia, mainly adultery and alcoholism for the parents, shoplifting and hot rods for the kids. Here, in Paradise Hills, Arizona, it's lights out. There aren't even crickets. In the first line of the movie, a disembodied voice-over from Christian Slater, there's a question: "Did you ever get the feeling that everything in the United States is completely fucked up? You know that feeling that the whole country is like one inch away from saying, that's it, forget it?"

That's the echo—a sonic boom. Instantly, in the dead setting the film has established as nothing, you expect everything, and you're ready for anything. But instead of the arena of the Sixties—the place open to anyone to enter and be free—this is the voice of a secret culture.

It's set forth as a secret, like kids in the 1950s listening to Little Richard on their transistor radios under the covers late at night, not so much afraid their parents would tell them to go to sleep as dreamily celebrating the fact that they had a secret to keep, something of their own that they couldn't and wouldn't share. Christian Slater's voice comes out of a tiny, Radio Shack–built pirate radio station—no sudden cultural explosion, but a single high school kid trying to come to life.

Every night at ten, he switches on his equipment and starts talking. He plays records, talks over them, blathers on, maybe for five minutes, maybe for hours. He's got nice Sixties parents who wouldn't dream of asking him what he does under the covers. They know they have to give him what they're supposed to call his space.

Unlike a DJ from 1956 who screams and shouts as if the whole world is listening, this DJ imagines no one is listening. The Sixties principle of action was "The Whole World Is Watching," and that's what "We've gotta make the myths" is meant to signify—the idea that you could do something and it would immediately count, become a touchstone, something people would look back to as a saga of liberation, a tale told for generations. The line sounded stupid on the radio ads for the movie, but not in the movie itself: the film builds that arena. You hear Ray Manzarek tell Jim Morrison they've gotta make the myths, and it sounds like what anyone would want to do—it sounds like the only proper ambition.

But the kid in *Pump Up the Volume* has no arena, and the idea of actually appearing in public is unthinkable—worse, it's meaningless. There is no public. His parents give him his space, but there is no public space he might share with anyone else. As Margaret Thatcher once said with such satisfaction, her words nagging in Jenny Diski's head a generation later, "There is no such thing as society. There are individual men and women, and there are families." As a disc jockey, Christian Slater is a secret agent without a mission, a terrorist without an enemy. But in a world without an arena the fact that no one is listening is freedom. Because no one is listening, because nothing Slater says can have consequences, he can, with bright, dancing eyes behind his mask of a squint, say anything. He can discover what it is he wants to say.

That's the movie. That's what happens. Or rather that's where the story starts—the story that, really, doesn't happen.

A kid speaks; he becomes a rumor, then a craze among his fellow students, who haven't a clue who he is. He becomes their hero; they pass him by in the halls at school, never noticing the sad sack with his shoulders slumped. "I could be that anonymous nerd sitting across from you in chem lab," he says on the air one night; he gives them a taste of free speech. They organize themselves into an audience, into a crowd of fans, gathering every night in a parking lot to hear him, their car radios tuned to his signal, like a crowd filing into a concert hall to watch someone else be free.

But other listeners begin to act differently, without a purpose, with nothing more than the new notion that the life they've been given isn't what they want. Small acts of rebellion take place—grafitti on the school walls. They seem pro forma, secondhand. In a certain way *Pump Up the Volume* is no more than a 1990s version of a 1950s prom-crisis movie: the kids want to have a rock 'n' roll band at the big dance and the adults won't let them; at the end Bill Haley and the Comets show up, looking older than the parents, and everything turns out all right. But in *Pump Up the Volume* there are also small acts of rebellion that you know will change the lives of those who perform them, and leave them forever unrepentant and unsatisfied. "Did you ever get so sick of being told—" "Sick to *death*," answers one of Slater's listeners, the nicest girl in school—that's the role she's been raised to play. She puts her jewelry in the microwave and watches it blow up. She appears the next night at a school board meeting called to deal with the radio menace and speaks. She has a bandage over her nose; the film doesn't tell you if she was hit by a piece of flying microwave glass or if her father beat her up.

That's less important than the fact of someone standing up in front of a crowd, in front of people she used to be afraid of, and saying what she has to say, when days before she didn't know she had anything to say. This is a transforming experience: once you've dared to stand up in public and say what others perhaps don't want to hear, you will be changed. After that, you'll be braver—or you will remember that, once, you acted bravely, and forever after feel cowardly, but not like nothing. Not as if nothing is at stake; not as if it doesn't matter if you keep silent or speak out. It can happen at public meetings, where people in the crowd suddenly feel as if they don't recognize the person speaking, someone they've known for years or all their lives, because no one ever thought she had a thought in her head; it can happen on a stage, when a performer, knowing exactly what the people in the crowd expect, what they're there for, refuses to give it to them, and gives them something else.

Pump Up the Volume ends with mandated melodrama. The forces of order close in around the pirate station: the FCC, the school board, the school administration. Christian Slater and his co-conspirator Samantha Mathis are chased by a government helicopter; he's arrested, dragged into a police van. He waves to the crowd that's gathered to hear him, and then there's a freeze frame.

You don't know what will happen next, said the freeze frame at the end of François Truffaut's *The 400 Blows* in 1959. Over the decades the device itself froze, into cliché, until it came to mean the opposite: it's over, now you can leave, it never happened, it was just a movie, now it all stops.

But that isn't how *Pump Up the Volume* really ends. The screen goes black after the freeze, and then voices come on: two, three, four, multiplying, talking on top of each other, fading in and out, one secret, pirate disc jockey after another, male and female, from Maine to California and everywhere in between, each one saying, *Hello—no one knows what's going to happen next, me least of all.*

It's a corny ending. It's a fantasy. It's the conceit of one Sixties person, Allan Moyle, who wrote and directed the film. The scene broke my heart and sparked it, which is what corny endings are supposed to do: it made real something that is not. But it wasn't empty; it wasn't automatic. The most crucial, corniest line rang true to me: Samantha Mathis telling the DJ, in words that would echo through the country nearly twenty years later, when Barack Obama ran for president, "*You're* the voice you were waiting for."

In certain moments in the Doors' best music—in, say, the last slow, inexorably quieting minute of "The End"—you can hear one person believing that what he has to say is worth the time others might take to listen. Then it all vanishes; that person leaves the stage and never comes back.

The Sixties are most generously described as a time when people took part—when they stepped out of themselves and acted in public, as people who didn't know what would happen next, but who were sure that acts of true risk and fear would produce something different from what they had been raised to take for granted. You can find that spirit in the early years of the Civil Rights movement, where some people paid for their wish to act with their lives, and you can find it in certain songs. But the Sixties were also a time when people who could have acted, and even those who did, or believed they did, formed themselves into an audience that most of all wanted to watch. "The Whole World Is Watching" was a stupid irony: people went into the streets, they shouted, gave speeches, surrounded buildings, blocked the police, and then rushed home to watch themselves on the evening news, to be an audience for their own actions. I did it like anyone else. It seemed like a natural thing to do.

Pump Up the Volume faces this possibility, and in idealism and fantasy rejects it. Against the Sixties carnival, it insists on a desert, geographically and culturally, literally and metaphorically, and says that where there seems to be nothing, something new can appear. It posits a trivial setting—one nowhere high school, the setting of such tepid, already-made post-1950s, post-1960s high school movies as *Footloose* or *Rock 'n' Roll High School*—and says that out of this trivial setting can come people who are not trivial, people who the setting was never meant to make.

What does it mean to make cultural history? It means to make images and sounds, to launch ideas and sensations that feel absolutely new even if they are not. Cultural history is a matter of old forms dressed in new clothes that turn history in a new direction. Cultural history may mean to triumph—to achieve worldwide and enduring fame, even to affect the lives of countless people long after you are gone, as the Doors did; more likely it means to find yourself stranded in the history that goes on without you, incapable of killing, in yourself, the notion that things could be better, or merely different, more alive, than they are, which may have been what Jim Morrison saw when, that night in Miami in 1969, he looked out at the people in the crowd and told them, "You're all a bunch of fucking idiots! Letting people tell you what you're going to do! Letting people push you around! How long do you think it's going to last? How long are you going to let it go on? How long are you going to let them push you around? How long? Maybe you like it, maybe you like being pushed around. Maybe you love it, maybe you love getting your face stuck in the shit. Come on. You love it, don't you. You love it. You're all a bunch of slaves." People cheered and laughed; they thought it was part of the act, part of the show. Finally, with the band keeping a count behind him, Morrison tried to go back to the song he'd started with, until he couldn't anymore.

Gina Arnold, "Fools Rush In," *East Bay Express*, March 8, 1991, 47.

Eve Babitz, "Jim Morrison Is Alive and Well and Living in Hollywood," *Esquire*, March 1991.

Elvis Costello, quoted in Mark Rowland, "Strange Bedfellows" (joint interview with Jerry Garcia), *Musician*, March 1991, 57.

Ian McEwan, *The Innocent* (New York: Doubleday, 1990).

Paul Williams, "Rothchild Speaks," *Crawdaddy!* March 1967. Collected in Williams, *Outlaw Blues: A Book of Rock Music* (1969) (Glen Ellen, CA: Entwhistle, 2000).

Kim Gordon, "'I'm Really Scared When I Kill in My Dreams,'" *Artforum*, January 1983, 55.

Dave DiMartino, "'Uh-Oh, I Think I Exposed Myself Out There'" (quoting himself from an article published 1981), *BAM*, March 8, 1991.

When the Music's Over

A T COBO HALL, in Detroit, in 1970, the band kicks off a
song with what Jon Landau, writing in *Rolling Stone* in
1968, called "aimless, washed-out organ music." "Waaaaal,
we're gonna stop the show. Gonna stop the show," Jim Morrison says, and the band stops. "Hello, Detroit." Ray Manzarek
plays the organ equivalent of a rim shot behind Henny Young-
man. "Hello, Salt Lake. Hello, Washington, D.C. How ya
doin'." Robby Krieger does the same. "Minneapolis, how ya
doin'? Hey, Seattle—nice to *see ya*. Dallas, Texas. Hi, y'all."

"This was a device Jim used to keep the audience from becoming too comfortable," Krieger said in 1997. "He wanted
them to have that feeling 'something's wrong, something's not
quite right.'"

It was an instinct Morrison followed from the start. On Jan-uary 6, 1967, the Doors played their first show in San Fran-cisco, at the Fillmore Auditorium. *The Doors* had yet to be released. Not even a rumor in the Bay Area, they were third-billed under the Young Rascals and Sopwith Camel, a forgot-ten local band with one cute hit, "Hello Hello." "We get up on stage, and Bill Graham introduces us," Ray Manzarek said almost forty years later. "'We've got this band from Los Ange-les . . .' And people are booing Los Angeles," which is what people in San Francisco automatically did: Los Angeles was cheap, it was plastic, it was money, it was Hollywood, it was fake, and it made San Francisco seem like both a small town and the last outpost of civilization and good manners. "We come on stage and Jim says, '"When the Music's Over." Play "When the Music's Over."' I said, 'Why are we gonna start with "When the Music's Over"? It's a long song, it's slow. We want to just get onstage and kill them with "Break on Through."' Jim said, 'No, I've got a feeling, man. Put every-thing you can into your playing' . . . and it just exploded."

This was before audiences were too cool to show up for third-billed bands, or taunted anyone who wasn't headlining: people were curious. New bands were appearing and dis-appearing by the day; you never knew when a show might be a historic marker, a dividing line between past and future, or a last chance. Still, fourteen or fifteen minutes of a wandering piece of music that barely was a song, random phrases and passages of near silence heading in no apparent direction, pre-tentious pronouncements ("What have they done to the earth? What have they done to our fair sister?") and self-consciously poetic imagery ("I want to hear / The scream of the butterfly") punctuated mainly by convincingly psychotic screams—if anything was likely to produce walkouts, this was. Unless the first notes of the thing went straight through you and ricocheted back again from the other side, leaving you feeling as if your legs were water, which those notes could do.

The piece appeared on record nine months after *The Doors*, in September 1967, closing out *Strange Days*.* There were strong songs all across the record—"Strange Days," "Love Me Two Times," "Unhappy Girl," "People Are Strange." "My Eyes Have Seen You" was a driverless car revving its engine, cutting its gas, the engine revved higher, the gas cut again, the engine revving again and then the whole machine tearing down the strip as if it were the only car on the road, then taking Dead Man's Curve as if it were John Henry, blasting right through it.

But there was a lack of weight, an absence of seriousness. Rock 'n' roll, anyone would tell you, wasn't supposed to be serious, wasn't supposed to have weight, unless it was heavy, but if the music with which the Doors announced themselves said

---

*"One of the minor problems we had back in those days," the disc jockey Larry Miller says, speaking of his time at KMPX in San Francisco, where, originally holding down the midnight-to-6-a.m. shift on an otherwise all foreign-language station, he invented FM rock 'n' roll radio, "was that certain long songs turned into 'phone monsters.' Like 'Inagaddadivida.' Listeners to rock music were blown away by hearing anything more than three minutes long. There were good phone monsters, like the Stones' 'Goin' Home,' or Quicksilver's 'The Fool.' But after the umpteenth demand for 'When the Music's Over' and 'The End,' I decided one night I'd play them both—simultaneously.

"They are not just in different keys—they are in keys that clash badly. The result was like Charles Ives on acid.

"The demands for both songs diminished somewhat after that." (E-mail to GM, June 27, 2011).

anything, it said it wasn't kidding. There was a seriousness of intent that was thrilling on its own terms. There was a sense of consequences: to walk through the dramas being enacted on *The Doors* was to take a chance, just a chance, that you might not come out quite the same. That was what people wanted; that was what they hoped for; that was why they listened. That seductive promise was what they heard.

As *Strange Days* reached its last track, the first simple, hesitant, jerky organ notes changed the tone. They promised that this would not be rushed, that it would not be over soon, that the song was writing a check only it could cash. And it didn't pay off. It didn't sustain the suspense of its first moments, but that suspense lingered. It sent listeners back to the song to see if it would give up something that wasn't there the first, third, tenth time before, and it sent the band back to it too, to find out what all those minutes—eleven on record, always more on a stage—were for. In 1969, the Rolling Stones would answer: in many ways, with those slithering first notes building on themselves, each one catching the one before it and passing it, only to be caught in turn, until a broken guitar chord tipped the song into the harsh, unforgiving cauldron that for the next four minutes boiled over, "Gimmie Shelter" was the ultimate Doors record.

Some nights, "When the Music's Over" was a flat, featureless landscape, without intimations that anything worth remembering might be coming—and it was in such a setting that the song could generate drama from within itself. One night in 1968, in Houston, the piece was all but shapeless as it began. Morrison is clear and direct, but there's a song inside the song, and that's what he's after. At its most effective, the band is barely present at all, as if to give the singer the room he needs to wander out of his own, written words. "Confusion . . . confusion . . . confusion," he croons, trying to make the word, the idea, open a door. He follows "confusion" with "delusion." The pauses between words or musical phrases, with no change in tempo or volume, create a kind of airborne swamp, a miasma, that seems complete and whole. Manzarek taps a bump-bump-bump pattern on his bass keyboard, a dozen times, it could be a hundred times, so dully you don't notice it, unless you're trapped by it, and begin to count off the notes, unable to hear anything else. Here, "Sat up all night, talking and smoking, count the dead and wait for morning," sneaking into the song from the side, unbidden and un-written—*Not on the record!* some in the crowd will say to themselves, confused, *Aren't they supposed to play the record?*—is all the song wants.

The performance is so sure of itself, so confident, that, if they want it to, the song can say anything. It becomes an open field of action, and what the band holds back carries as great a charge as what it puts on the field. "Hey, look," Morrison says at one point, just before a written, recorded line—and the feeling is so conversational, so ordinary, that for an instant the performance vanishes, and even as the song goes on you can see him in the crowd which is no longer a crowd, just some people hanging around, asking them, What do you think? Is this working, is it happening? Why did you come tonight? Why are you here? Then he gets back onto the stage and, as on *Strange Days* in its last moments, takes the song back to that opening promise, that first apprehension of portent and dread. "When the music's over"—was it "Turn out the lights," or "Turn up the lights"? Night to night, city to city, year to year, it wasn't the same.

"Hello to the Cities," from "The Future Ain't What It Used to Be," in *The Doors Box Set* (Elektra, 1997).

Robby Krieger quoted in notes to *The Doors Box Set* (Elektra, 1997), 34.

Ray Manzarek quoted in *The Doors with Ben Fong-Torres, The Doors* (New York: Hyperion, 2006), 73.

"When the Music's Over," *Strange Days* (Elektra, 1967).

——, Sam Houston Coliseum, Houston, July 10, 1968, collected on *Boot Yer Butt! The Doors Bootlegs* (Rhino Handmade, 2003).

The Crystal Ship

W<small>HO WRITES MOST</small> of your songs?" the late Greg Shaw asked the Doors in San Francisco in 1967, just after the band's March dates at the Matrix, a congenial little box of a club. "Jim writes most of the lyrics," Robby Krieger said. "I noticed that some of your songs are very strange, like 'The End' and 'Moonlight Drive' and a few others," Shaw said. "A strong mood of death running through a lot of them. I mean, it almost seems as if you lost your mind once, sometime in your past, with these songs as the result. I get the impression from like, 'End of the Night' particularly a real feeling of Celine, *Journey to the End of the Night,* and from 'The End' and many of the other songs, of the *Tibetan Book of the Dead.* Really strong moods." "I don't know," Jim Morrison said. "Compared to some of the stuff I've heard in San Francisco, I don't think it's too strange. It's pretty straight stuff."

"The streets are fields that never die," from "The Crystal Ship," from *The Doors*, a song the band played at the Matrix, was a captivating image; so was "Speak in secret alphabets," from "Soul Kitchen," also from *The Doors*, which they played right before "The Crystal Ship." As images they hovered, and as ideas, they rang. On the page, maybe as you let them play in your head, they seemed transparent, to explain themselves immediately, but as Jim Morrison sang them, they didn't.

Greg Shaw was right about death. Who knew what shore Morrison's crystal ship, or his own ship, was headed for? Listening now to the ineffable take of the song from *The Doors*, and to the more insistent, expansive performance from the Matrix, the song is pitched between dream and waking, speech and silence, fantasy and act, death or the next morning. It doesn't light. Morrison's balance over the weightless, hesitating figures in the music—the first two words of the song let out in the echoing silence of an empty house; a swooping, sealing bass note; Ray Manzarek's high, slipstream organ; most of all, the stoic, wrap-it-up climb in John Densmore's repeating sets of taps on his snare or cymbal to mark the shift from one movement, one point of view, to the next—calls up a sleepwalker on a tightrope. The physical body of the performance is that of a single breath exhaled across two and a half minutes, and it could be a last breath.

The oddness of the first words—"Before you slip into unconsciousness"—

> *Be*
>   *fore*
>   *you*
>   *slip*
> *into*
> *unconsciousness*

—throws you off, pulls you down, right from the start. This could be sleep, it could be an overdose, inflicted by the singer or the person he's addressing; it could be murder, suicide, or a suicide pact. Or simply someone about to pass out drunk. From beginning to end—the floating drift across the music— Morrison presents the situation with absolute equanimity. He raises his voice, his volume, only once, near the end, when he sings the title of the song as if he's just discovered it: the three words, the perfect metaphor, the Flying Dutchman of the heart.

Morrison's voice was never more modest, never more full. He was never a soul singer—the reserve of someone thinking everything over, thinking everything through, kept him from that—but here he gave himself up to the steps of the song, steps made of images, notes, melody most of all, trusting those steps to lead to somewhere worth going, even if there was no hint where that might be. "Sometimes I make up words so I can remember the melody I hear," Morrison once said; you can hear that happening here.

Inside this soft, comforting, deeply elegant song, what Raymond Chandler called the big sleep, what Ross Macdonald called the chill, lingered, lay back on a bed with its lips parted, strolled naked through the rooms of the song like Evan Rachel Wood in Todd Haynes's 2011 film of James M. Cain's *Mildred Pierce*. Death was more distant in "The Crystal Ship" than in "End of the Night," farther on on *The Doors*, and more convincing. "End of the Night" made a gorgeous setting for Blake's "Some are born to sweet delight / Some are born to endless night," so gorgeous you could think that to make that setting was the only reason for writing the song. The band let the lines echo in the sound, but not in the heart, as they would when Gary Farmer's Nobody spoke them almost thirty years later in Jim Jarmusch's *Dead Man*, and "The Crystal Ship" was sailing for the heart or nowhere.

In 2007 the Whitney Museum of American Art in New York opened its fortieth-anniversary *Summer of Love—Art of the Psychedelic Era* retrospective; there was a huge catalogue, the cover spelling out the magic words in a psychedelically unreadable design, recalling those halcyon days when thousands made the pilgrimage to San Francisco to be attacked by the police, dance in the streets, buy drugs, get raped and robbed, and hear wonderful music. Rhino Records released *Love Is the Song We Sing*, a four-CD set that caught the Summer of Love principally by collecting crummy singles by Psychedelic-Era San Francisco Bay Area bands. Nothing would have been more out of place than the sweep, the grandeur, the calmness of the Doors.

San Francisco music was soft at the center—Jefferson Airplane passed out buttons reading JEFFERSON AIRPLANE LOVES YOU and the Grateful Dead didn't believe in death at all. San Francisco music did believe in happy endings. Not all of it. On the first album from Moby Grape, in 1967, a band all but ridden out of town for violating the bohemian vow of visible poverty by accepting a huge promotional campaign by Columbia, there were the warnings of "Lazy Me" ("I'll just lay here, and decay here") and the rising doubts of "Indifference," the promise of the Haight-Ashbury at just that point where it turned into a curse. There was the breakdown of Moby Grape leader Skip Spence two years later, with *Oar*, a cracked, scattered, stumblebum travelogue that took you back and forth between the campfire and the psycho ward. The singer stood on the street, with open sores he didn't know he was scratching, clothes filthy, talking to someone who wasn't there; in every broken tune there was a memory of what could have been, a damn for what should have, when all that was left was what never was.

There was the Great Society, captured, on *Love Is the Song We Sing*—it's embarrassing to keep typing the phrase—at a performance at the Matrix in 1966, when Grace Slick was a sometime model and full-time bohemian with a daring band behind her. With Jefferson Airplane she would make "Somebody to Love" a huge national hit in 1967—all triumph, a soaring escape. A year before it was just the big number of a group that rarely topped the bill at the ballrooms: a fearsome, frightening challenge. Called "Someone to Love" then, it was "Like a Rolling Stone" stripped of its carnival metaphors: if you find yourself on your own, like a complete unknown, what are you going to do then? Die doped-up and gang-banged in a crash pad a block off the Haight, or live a new life? The band finds a fierce rhythmic count to step up the tension—the pressure—between each chorus and the next verse, a breach that seems to open up the ground beneath their feet, and Slick comes off of it every time more outraged, disgusted, contemptuous of anyone who doesn't have the courage to face the truth, throw away the past, and not look back. It's staggering: you've walked into this dodgy little place and here's this nice-looking person on the stage all but threatening you with a spiritual death penalty, and turning you into a jury that convicts yourself.

There is a sullen, hateful, dangerous edge in the music—when Slick says "the garden flowers all are dead," they are dead—an edge muffled in the music everyone else made. Only the Great Society brought it to the surface, for a few months thrilled by the chance to ask a question no one wanted to answer: how do you get from here to nowhere?

It was a kind of heedless prophecy. The Great Society—
which sometimes billed themselves as the Great!! Society!!—
didn't want to hear the bad answers: who would? But they
were there in their music, and you can hear so much of the fa-
bled San Francisco Sound, today, as an effort to fight off the
sorts of stories implicit in the music of Moby Grape, Skip
Spence, the Great Society, and the Doors. I think of a forgotten novel called *Loose Jam*, by one Wayne Wilson. It came
out in 1990; when I listen to Skip Spence, Grace Slick, the
Doors, it comes right back.

In Morro Bay, a town a little under two hundred miles
south of San Francisco, a fat, balding man named Henry has a
nothing job, an embarrassment for a guy on the edge of forty,
but he's not complaining. Then his old pal Miles shows up.
Miles—Henry's Vietnam buddy and former bandleader, a
one-legged, one-time Voice of a Generation, turns Henry's
world upside down without half trying. He's more irritating
than compelling—the reader wants him to leave even more
than Henry does. What is compelling is the inexorable slide of
the narrative from orderly, structured occurrences into chaos:
a sort of match from the artistry and confidence at the beginning of that first Moby Grape album—the thrilling charge of
"Fall on You" and "Omaha"—to the hidden corners and dark-
ened rooms at the end of the album, the people who walked
off the record into rooms worse than that.

Very quickly, Henry's hard-won belief that life is governed
by some inherent, given set of limits—a belief won through
countless defeats, compromises, and willful refusals to remember a life that promised anything else—seems impossible
to credit. As the present breaks up—Henry's job lost, his house
wrecked, his would-be girlfriend stolen—Vietnam returns in

flashbacks, and you begin to recognize Henry clutching for the underside of middle-class gentility as a version of Hemingway's Nick Adams, hanging on to his fishing pole in "Big Two-Hearted River" in the aftermath of the First World War. But as it is portrayed here, Vietnam was—is—not a war but a charnel house. It's not a situation constructed to realize some geopolitical objective, but a situation constructed to strip off all morality, all constraint, and not at anyone's My Lai, but back at camp, among one's fellows, as the urge to murder seeks its closest target. Such celebrated Vietnam novels as Tim O'Brien's *Going After Cacciato* or memoirs on the order of Philip Caputo's *A Rumor of War* were fundamentally, no matter how phonily, about ethics; Wayne Wilson wasn't interested. In his accounts of meaningless conflicts between people supposedly on the same side, you're returned to the worst moment in Joseph Heller's *Catch-22*, Aarfy's rape and murder of Michaela, the Italian servant girl, except that that was a signal event, impossible for a reader to forget, and what happens in Wilson's Vietnam—ordinary life reduced to the level of the sort of obscene insult that leaves a person weak, humiliated, and ready to kill whoever looks ready to die—is hard to remember, a black haze, and as terrifying as a Bosch painting of hell.

Soon enough, as Henry and Miles's flight from Miles's pursuer, an enemy from Vietnam, puts them on the road, the language of flashbacks takes over the present. A long-ago night of sordid, back-to-the-world Haight-Ashbury hippie sex gets payback: people who once thought they were living out the zeitgeist return as flotsam, garbage tossed up decades later. As they return, they change old horrors, even decent memories, into a simple seediness. People just get uglier, and a sense of time is the last thing they can use: "Henry was astonished at the contrast between this haggard woman and the girl to whom he'd surrendered on that night so long ago"—he can't even think about what he must look like to her. "Now the corners of her mouth sagged and the skin below her eye looked bruised and when Henry bent to kiss the top of her head a vapor of beer and fried onions rose from her hair . . . Some mangy dog with a red bandana tied around its neck (Henry was willing to bet its name was something like Kilo or Shit) followed them into the living room." The dog's name turns out to be Roach.

If all of that—the Skip Spence story, Henry's story, the back door Grace Slick flung open after you walked through the front door—isn't present in "The Crystal Ship," it is, along with other lives, waiting. The glamour in the song hides its demons, but doesn't banish them.

At the Matrix, the tale unwinds in a swaying wind. Morrison waits behind the words, as if letting them emerge of their own accord, at their own speed. Kicked off by what feels like a spontaneous, joyous *Heyyyyyy!* from Morrison, Manzarek's organ solo is full of color, the sound rising to the low ceiling and spreading out from there, driven by the thrill of getting it right, of the band truly finding its voice for the first time that night—and, as it happened, the last.

The words, the image of "the crystal ship" is propelled out of the song, launched into its black sea. Morrison embraces the words, the image, as if it's always been a treasure to him, and it is instantly lit. As he heads for the end of the song— "When we get back, I'll drop a line," a wave goodbye that for me has always called up Robert Johnson's "When I return / You'll have a great long story to tell," a scene full of affection, regret, a scene that leaves the listener wondering if the person singing and the person to whom he's speaking will ever see each other again—its first moment returns. "Before you . . ."— there seems to be no assurance that any words will follow, and no need for them at all.

"Interview with the Doors," *Mojo-Navigator Rock + Roll News* no. 14, August 1967. Collected in Suzy Shaw and Mick Farren, *BOMP!—Saving the World One Record at a Time* (Pasadena: AMMO Books, 2007), 80.

"The Crystal Ship," *The Doors* (Elektra, 1967).

———, *Live at the Matrix* (DMC/Rhino, 2008).

Jim Morrison, in John Densmore, *Riders on the Storm: My Life with Jim Morrison and the Doors* (New York: Delacorte, 1990), 59: "Jim was a guy with a natural instinct for melody but no knowledge of chords to hang it on."

Moby Grape, *Moby Grape* (Columbia, 1967). See the fine retrospective *Vintage: The Very Best of Moby Grape* (Columbia Legacy, 1993).

Skip Spence, *Oar* (Columbia, 1969). The 2000 reissue on Sundazed includes ten additional tracks and my *Rolling Stone* review of the album upon its release. The original album supposedly sold fewer copies than any LP release in Columbia history, and was out of print within a year; it was recorded in Nashville, with Spence as a one-man band (the original drummer in the Jefferson Airplane, he played guitar in Moby Grape), after he spent months in Bellevue following a psychotic breakdown: he tried to attack his bandmates Jerry Miller and Don Stevenson with an axe.

Great Society, "Someone to Love," recorded at the Matrix, summer 1966. Originally released on *Conspicuous Only in Its Absence* (Columbia, 1968, the band's first, posthumous album; see also *Born to Be Burned*, Sundazed, 1995, which includes the single version of "Someone to Love," released February 1966 on the Northbeach label); collected on *Love Is the Song We Sing: San Francisco Nuggets 1965–1970* (Rhino, 2007), which along with wonderful photographs and early and signal recordings by Big Brother and the Holding Company, Country Joe and the Fish, Jefferson Airplane, Quicksilver Messenger Service, the Charlatans, Moby Grape, and the Grateful Dead, also features perhaps the only readily available proof that Blackburn and Snow, Wild-flower, the Frantics, the Front Line, the Mourning Reign, the Oxford Circle, the Stained  Glass, the Otherside, Teddy and His Patches, the Immediate Family, the New Breed, People, the Generation, Butch Engle and the Styx ("Hey I'm Lost"—no kidding), Country Weather, Public Nuisance, and the Savage Resurrection existed at all.

Wayne Wilson, *Loose Jam* (New York: Delacorte, 1990). See also Charles Perry, *The Haight-Ashbury: A History* (New York: Random House/Rolling Stone Press, 1984); Joel Selvin's harrowing *The Summer of Love: The Inside Story of LSD, Rock & Roll, Free Love, and High Times in the Wild West* (New York: Dutton, 1994); and Barney Hoskyns's incandescent if rosy *Beneath the Diamond Sky: Haight-Ashbury 1965–1970* (London: Bloomsbury, 1997).

Robert Johnson, "From Four Until Late" (1937). Best heard on *The Centennial Collection—The Complete Recordings* (Columbia Legacy, 2011).

Soul Kitchen

FROM THE TIME the Doors first came together in Venice in 1965 — at first, Ray Manzarek, his brother Rick on guitar, his brother Jim on harmonica, Jim Morrison, and John Densmore — they loosened up with "Gloria," like a thousand other garage bands around the country, jumping on Them's greatest hit when they got tired of kicking off with "Louie Louie." As Don Henley once said, reviewing the all-author band the Rock Bottom Remainders at their debut at the 1992 American Booksellers Association convention in Anaheim, "It's hard to fuck up 'Gloria'" — that just before detailing just how the Remainders had achieved the nearly impossible. From the beginning, though, the Doors also made "Gloria" part of their shows. Soon after winning the spot as house band at the Whisky à Go-Go in May 1966, opening for Captain Beefheart, Love, and Buffalo Springfield, they found themselves second on the bill to Them itself. Their leader, Van Morrison, had claimed "Gloria" as the first song he ever wrote, two years before in Belfast, when Them, the house band at the Maritime Hotel, would play it for twenty minutes or more—he couldn't know in 1966 that it would follow him for the rest of his life, just like "Light My Fire" would always follow the Doors.

On the last night of a two-week stand, the Doors and Them took the stage together, first for Wilson Pickett's "In the Midnight Hour," which had become the classy "Louie Louie" for groups with any pretensions toward rock 'n' roll as an art form. One night that same year in San Francisco, at the Fillmore, Quicksilver Messenger Service ended their set with "In the Midnight Hour," the Grateful Dead ended theirs with it, Jefferson Airplane ended theirs with it ("Not a classic, but an epic," Jon Landau had written of Pickett's 1965 original, as if it were something to test yourself against, not beat to death), until finally, somewhere around two in the morning, all three bands climbed onto the stage again and tried to ride the exhausted beast one more time. At the Whisky, the two Morrisons, Them and the Doors, faced off together for "Gloria." The pictures from that night show Van Morrison as a dervish, his eyes rolling like dice, with Jim Morrison towering above him, not moving, his eyes closed. Really, he could be praying the words—"Like to tell you about my baby / You know she comes around / About five feet four / From her head to the ground"—waiting for the chance to sing, to come in, maybe, on "Just about midnight."

The respect you can see in Jim Morrison's face was still there when the Doors played "Gloria" at the Matrix nine months later to close a night; so is a proud, grungy garage sound, at first only drums and guitar, letting the song find its

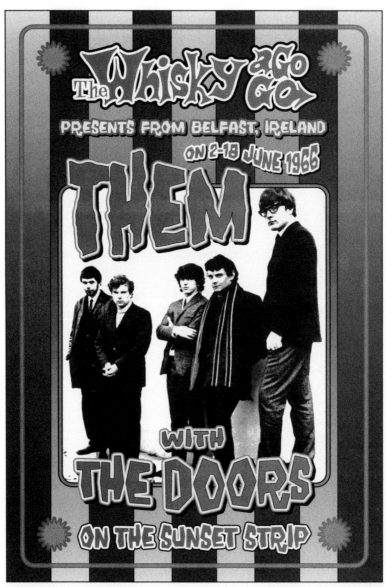

footing. There's no attempt to pump the song up, to make it more than it is: "And her name is *G! L! O*—" Even when Jim Morrison shifts the language, for the first verse dropping the third line and part of the fourth, dropping "Just about five feet four / From her—" so that the song opens, as for the Doors it always would—

Tell you about my baby
She comes around
She comes around here
Head to the ground

—making an image of surpassing strangeness, a woman so stooped she's bent in half, or crawling on the ground, if not listening with her ear to the ground for some signal that the time is right; the song retains its moral shape, its essential modesty, even when the singer is shouting out the name, even when everyone in the band is shouting, even when the singer screams that she makes him feel alright. The song held its shape when Jim Morrison shifted its terrain, from Van Morrison's room in Belfast to Robert Johnson's Mississippi—

You got to meet me at the crossroads
You got to meet me at the edge of town
Outskirts of the city
You better come alone
Just you and I
And the evening sky

—and it held its shape even when Jim Morrison, as Van Morrison almost dares any other singer of the song to do, has to take it past Van Morrison's "She knock upon my door / She comes in my room" to "Closer, closer / Touch me, baby, *touchhhhhh me*," even "Eat it," if that's what he says, falling back from whatever it is he's singing, putting the lightest question mark at the end of whatever word it is. Manzarek closes it with a keening, lyrical wham.

In 1969, in Los Angeles after the Miami disaster, at a sound check, the Doors sound like Paul Revere and the Raiders at their best: a crackling, soulful guitar, a hoarse vocal, the band playing with nothing to prove, letting the song play them, Densmore, Robby Krieger, and Manzarek coming in for the chorus, as if it's not three people but a choir chanting "GLO-HHHHHHHH *RIA!*" as Morrison counts off the letters. Then the tune breaks, and it turns. "You were my queen, and I was your fool / Riding home, after school," Morrison croons. "It's getting softer," he says, half in imitation of the Isley Brothers' "A little bit softer now" in "Shout," half asking the song to give him the time he needs. "A little bit softer now / Slow it down." The band brings the song to a crawl. "Wrap your legs around my neck," Morrison asks, trying to sound lascivious, asking for more, until finally she does make him feel alright: "It's getting harder." And then "it's getting too fast." And then it's "too late, too late, too late, too late," he's come too fast, maybe before he's even inside, and there's nothing left to do but shout out that name again, bigger than ever, and get out with an ending that feels bigger than anything that came before.

It was a performance that, with no audience, with no one to care, to mull it over, to pick it apart, crossed over into priapic self-parody and instantly crossed back into impotent self-loathing, but at the end still allowed the song to sound like itself. But by the time the Doors settled in for a week of shows in New York in 1970, and a kind of war between the band and its audience was under way, a war whose weapons were contempt on both sides, there was nothing left of the song but the porn movie it had always half promised to be.

"Getting softer," Morrison whispered in New York, now more like Jerry Lee Lewis in "Whole Lotta Shakin' Goin' On." The band slows. "Take it," Morrison sings. "Eat it. Lick it. Put your lips around my cock, baby." "SUCK IT!" Manzarek snaps from the side, sounding like someone who's paying to watch. "Gonna eat you, honey," Morrison sways. "TASTE IT!" says Manzarek. "Getting harder, harder, longer," Morrison warbles, too early for *South Park: Bigger, Longer & Uncut*. It goes on, with Manzarek adding a wolf whistle after Morrison's "Wrap your hair around my skin."

"Getting harder," Morrison announces again. "HARDER," Manzarek seconds, as if the point needs to be stressed. "Getting faster too," Morrison says, doubt behind the bravado. "GETTING LONGER!" says Manzarek. "It's getting too darn fast," Morrison says, the *darn* sticking out, as if this is a little boy not ready for grown-up words. "It's getting harder, gonna rip you in two, woo!"—and nothing happens. The singer pulls the rug out from under himself, pulls the song inside out: "Too late, too late, can't stop—"

Plainly, the band loved the song too much to ever let it go, no matter how traduced at their hands it might become: always, there was that clattering beginning, with Krieger battering his strings as if his fingers were sticks, and that colossal finish, Manzarek running the flourishes he was so fond of right into a wall. Just as plainly, the song got under Jim Morrison's skin; it wouldn't let him go. But "Gloria" gave the Doors something back.

"Soul Kitchen" was the Doors' own "Gloria"—with the same steady climb toward a looming chorus. It was a staircase—not, as with "Gloria," in imagery, but in the cadence the two songs shared, slowed down so strongly in "Soul Kitchen" that a sense of deliberation, so physical that it was more body than thought, became the guiding spirit of the song.

The first ambitious piece of writing on rock 'n' roll I recall reading was Paul Williams's "Rock Is Rock: A Discussion of a Doors Song," in the May 1967 issue of *Crawdaddy!* To Williams, "Soul Kitchen" wasn't "Gloria," it was "Blowin' in the Wind," and just as "Blowin' in the Wind" had a message— to Williams, that the answer, knowledge, is beyond our reach—so did "Soul Kitchen": "The message of 'Soul Kitchen' is of course 'Learn to forget.'" It's a phrase that makes a hinge, almost exactly halfway through the song, as it appeared on *The Doors*.

Never mind that when people tell you that anything is a matter of *of course*—and especially anything having anything to do with art—they are telling you to stop thinking, to stop listening, to stop seeing, to shut up. "Soul Kitchen" does not have a message. It's an image, as quietly dramatic a sexual image as any could be. For all of Jim Morrison's unbearable poetic extravaganzas on Doors albums, those two words are poetry, translating something almost beyond words into ordinary language and back again to the ether—just as the line that carries the image, the moment of poetry, "Let me sleep all night in your soul kitchen," is intuitive songwriting, and the line that follows, "Warm my mind near your gentle stove," with its nicely matched kitchen and stove, is Scrabble. It doesn't hurt the ruling image, doesn't touch it: "soul kitchen" is too unlikely, too immediately right.

The song is pulled forward—pulled toward itself, what it wants, what it wants to be—by that image. "Speak in secret alphabets" is no less sexual, and no less sexual than Bob Seger's "Working on mysteries without any clues," but Seger, in "Night Moves" in 1976, looking back to 1962, when he was seventeen, was being true to his school, where "secret alphabets" would have got you laughed at. Jim Morrison, thinking of himself as a poet, could ask himself not merely how to say it, but how not to: how to say what you mean to say while saying many other things at the same time. "Oh, the wonder," Seger mouthed, giving up; "Speak in secret alphabets," Morrison chanted, eyes and hands running over bodies, bodies closing eyes and hands, until the music all but gave off scent. "Soul Kitchen" entered "Gloria"'s building, climbed its stairs, knocked on its door, went into its room, and flew out the window.

On record, the song is a dark room, the lights flicking off, the sign on the door switched from OPEN to CLOSED. But like every other Doors song, it changed shape according to the mood of the band, the city, the hall, the audience, the weather, the news, whether Morrison was in love with the song or consumed with hate for anyone else who claimed to love it, whether he was drunk or sober or just drunk enough not to care what anybody else thought. In Chicago, more than a year after *The Doors* began its climb to #2 on the charts, "Soul Kitchen" is a river; the point is not to cross it, but to let it take you down. Over more than seven and a half minutes, more than twice the length of the song on record, Morrison seems more interested in finding spaces in the song where he can get off of it, walk away, squint at the horizon, reciting the Lord's Prayer, than in his "Poor Otis, dead and gone, left me here to sing his song," which here does feel like a gesture of regret and comradeship, especially when he adds, from Lead Belly, from Ray Charles's "What'd I Say," from the old folk song "Liza Jane," "Pretty little girl with the red dress on . . . Poor Otis, dead and gone."

On *The Doors* the chorus comes back, hammering, where everything else was reverie, an elegy to a night over before it began, a fantasy that might yet be realized, through the night and into the next day, over the hill and through the woods. The song makes you wait for its two words, raised like hands over eyes, the fingers opening and closing.

Them, "Gloria" (London, 1965, #93).

Don Henley, "Amateur Night," *LA Weekly*, June 3–10, 1992. "It was a cacophonous frat-party nightmare," Henley wrote of the Rock Bottom Remainders' debut performance of "Louie Louie," at Cowboy Boogie in Anaheim on May 25, 1992. "Had we been in Texas, there would have been gatoring, chugging and hurling . . . Then the band staggered into 'Gloria,' with the lead vocal by Dave Barry. Back in the peace-and-love era I had to play 'Gloria' 13 times in one night at a Delta Sig party, so this song affects me like burnt pizza. Barry's late-'60s college-boy version of a Beatle haircut only fueled the memory. He took the usual liberties with the lyrics (the part about coming into the bedroom)."

Mid-Life Confidential: The Rock Bottom Remainders Tour America with Three Chords and an Attitude, ed. Dave Marsh (New York: Viking, 1994). With contributions by Dave Barry, Tad Bartimus, Roy Blount, Jr., Michael Dorris, Robert Fulghum, Kathi Goldmark, Matt Groening, Stephen King, Tabitha King, Barbara Kingsolver, Al Kooper, GM, Dave Marsh, Ridley Pearson, Joel Selvin, and Amy Tan. Featuring a long round-robin on possible perfect-crime responses to the Don Henley review, mostly involving

Rock Bottom Remainders, The Roxy, Atlanta, 1993
(left to right, front, Al Kooper, guitar, Critics Chorus wih Joel Selvin,
Dave Marsh, GM, Roy Blount, Jr., and guest; back, Dave Barry, guitar,
Josh Kelly, drums, Ridley Pearson, bass, Jimmy Vivino, keyboards)

arcane Chinese tortures and murder techniques, a photo of a blood-smeared Dave Marsh in a wig and a prom dress as the dead girlfriend in "Teen Angel," and Remainders' musical director Al Kooper (as the author of *Backstage Passes and Backstabbing Bastards,* not a ringer) on the Critics' Chorus: "This is the nadir of western civilization. Right here, in our show."

"Gloria," *Live at the Matrix* (DMC/Rhino, 2008).

———, Los Angeles, Aquarius Theatre, 1969, from *Alive She Cried* (Elektra, 1983), collected on *In Concert* (Elektra, 1991).

———, New York, Felt Forum, January 18, 1970, from "Live in New York," in *The Doors Box Set* (Elektra, 1997).

"Soul Kitchen," *The Doors* (Elektra, 1967).

———, Chicago Coliseum, May 10, 1968, collected on *Boot Yer Butt! The Doors Bootlegs* (Rhino Handmade, 2003).

Van Morrison and Jim Morrison at the Whisky. The best photos, by
   George Rodriguez, in smoky color, are in *The Doors with Ben
   Fong-Torres, The Doors* (New York: Hyperion, 2006), 56–57.
Paul Williams, "Rock Is Rock: A Discussion of a Doors Song,"
   Crawdaddy! May 1967. Collected in Williams, *Outlaw Blues: A
   Book of Rock Music* (1969) (Glen Ellen, CA: Entwhistle, 2000).
Bob Seger, "Night Moves" (Capitol, 1976, #4).

Light My Fire,
The Ed Sullivan Show,
1967

A ND YOU FELLAS, why don't you have a nice *smile* on your faces when you go out there?" said Ed Sullivan, backstage on September 17, 1967, just as the Doors were about to step in front of the cameras to play "Light My Fire." "There's no point in being *sullen*. You know what I mean?" "But we're a sullen group, Ed," said Ray Manzarek.

So he said in 1991 in Oliver Stones's *The Doors*, anyway. It was the site of the first national Doors scandal, or rather success-through-scandal: as with Bob Dylan and the Rolling Stones before them, the people running the show, broadcast live, wanted something other from the Doors than what they came to play. For Bob Dylan in 1963 it was "Talkin' John Birch Society Blues" the show wanted axed, and he walked off. For the Rolling Stones earlier in 1967 it was, all too famously, "Let's Spend the Night Together"; as they were told to do, Mick Jagger and Keith Richards sang "Let's spend some time together," with Mick popping his eyes to let the world know it was in on the joke.* For the Doors, CBS demanded they change the line "Girl, we couldn't get much higher"—supposedly, to "couldn't get much better." The network couldn't have contrived a less musical solution if they'd suggested Jim Morrison sing the chemical formula for lithium. Supposedly, the rest of the band was ready to acquiesce—*If it was good enough for the Stones . . .* This was a big deal; more dates were dangled. Supposedly, Morrison said okay.

It's hard to believe Manzarek, John Densmore, and Robby Krieger didn't know what was coming. Densmore begins the performance with the huge *stomp!* of a single shot on the snare—as someone said at the time, it was hard to imagine anyone hitting anything harder. But after that he hits everything else too hard. You don't hear a beat. You hear nerves, or fear.

Morrison steps into the song languidly, with no tension, no foreshadowing. Unlike Elvis Presley in his third and last appearance on the Sullivan show, in 1957, the only time he was shot from the waist up—with Elvis pointedly looking down at his own body, as if what the camera was now hiding was something he'd never showed when the camera was all the way

---

*In November 1955 Bo Diddley was booked, and told by Sullivan to sing Tennessee Ernie Ford's "Sixteen Tons," then the biggest song in the country. He did "Bo Diddley" instead and never appeared on the show again.

back, catching him from head to toe, he and his combo in action, playing to each other with joy, abandon, and speed—Morrison dropped no clues. He all but used the tune as a trampoline. "Girl, we couldn't get much hiiiii," he sang, letting the rest of *higher* disappear, letting it slip by as if it hadn't been there at all, and while at least the sign of the offending word had been present, going out to the nation live, you could believe that in fact this was okay: okay for CBS, an honorable compromise for the Doors. "FIGH-YARRRRGH! YEAH!" Morrison screamed just about a minute in, just before Manzarek begins a seven-second solo, squeezing the song into its single version, as if Morrison was making up for what wasn't there. His scream was exciting. Nothing else had been.

Morrison came off Manzarek's solo as smoothly as before. He sang the first verse. He passed over the melody, licking the word *fire* as Elvis himself might have done, if he'd closed his 1960 post-Army comeback album *Elvis Is Back!* with "Light My Fire" instead of "Reconsider Baby"—as if, given what Elvis did to Lowell Fulsom's signature song, infusing every word with a heat that has never cooled, there was any difference.

For the refrain Morrison screamed "FIRE!" again. And then he pulled out all the stops; listening, it sounds as if he's tearing off his clothes. His voice is suddenly rough, harsh, bearing down, an explosion of pressure. Densmore finds his footing, and gives Morrison his. It's a different song, a different night, a different place; a different audience is called into being. Now every breath is deep, drawn from all the way down in the chest, the breath you draw before you're about to leap; each breath is as strong, as sudden, as full of vengeance and lust as that moment when Densmore's stick first hit the skin.

Morrison's diction coarsens, the words lose their beginnings and endings, the singer is rushing past the song, the song is coming up behind the singer like a wave, they meet at Morrison's furious, inflamed *higher*, which here, with the song taking on its full body, carries no more musical or moral weight than any other word, note, phrase, sound—the sound, right now, of freedom. It's shocking, how much pleasure freedom can bring: *"Come on!"* Manzarek shouts from the side in the last chorus, beside himself. Now they're on the other side. After this, did the song ever need to be played again?

"Light My Fire," *The Ed Sullivan Show*, collected on *When You're Strange: Songs from the Motion Picture: A Film About The Doors* (DMC/Rhino, 2010).

Elvis Presley, *The Ed Sullivan Shows* (Image Entertainment DVD, 2006); notes by GM.

——, *Elvis Is Back!* (1960). The 2011 RCA Legacy reissue comprises two CDs, including also the 1960–61 singles "Fame and Fortune," "It's Now or Never," "A Mess of Blues," "Are You Lonesome Tonight?" and "Surrender," plus the 1961 album *Something for Everybody*, and the 1961–62 singles "I Feel So Bad," "(Marie's the Name) His Latest Flame," "Little Sister," and "Good Luck Charm." Like so many before and after him, Jim Morrison knew Elvis Presley had something no one else would ever have, which only made him reach for it more passionately, and more cryptically, in a manner less obvious, all but occulted. Given the delicacy and glamour Elvis gives the songs on *Elvis Is Back!* from "Fever" to "Girl of My Best Friend" to "Dirty, Dirty Feeling" to "Such a Night," it's hard to believe this wasn't the Elvis album Morrison played more than any other. Today you can hear him all over it.

The Unknown Soldier
in 1968

R AY WANTED JIM TO take it all the way," John Densmore
wrote in 1990, looking back in his book *Riders on the
Storm*. "To the White House. He imagined himself secretary
of state. Sounded like fantasy time to me, but I think a part of
Ray hoped it would really happen. I thought Jim was too crazy
to be as popular as he was already! I was scared by the idea of
more power in his hands." For Morrison himself, it wasn't altogether off his mind. "There should be a week of national
hilarity . . . a cessation of all work, all business, all discrimina-
tion, all authority," he said to his friend Jerry Hopkins, who
was interviewing Morrison for *Rolling Stone*. "A week of total
freedom. That'd be a start. Of course, the power structure
wouldn't really alter. But someone off the streets—I don't

know how they'd pick him, at random, perhaps—would become president. Someone else would become vice president. Others would be senators, congressmen, on the supreme court, policemen . . . One thing I said one time: the logical extension of the ego is God. I think the logical extension of living in America is to be President."

| | |

"THE UNKNOWN SOLDIER" is not much of a song. It has that hurdy-gurdy rhythm that allows for vocal improvisation but never really gets anywhere. The music remembers the elegant stop time, the careful, drunken steps—one step forward, a pause, a moment to think about it, another step—of "Alabama Song (Whisky Bar)" on the band's first album. Kurt Weill's 1927 attempt to be Bix Beiderbecke with Bertolt Brecht's little ditty, Lotte Lenya's attempt to be Bessie Smith or Sara Martin—writing and singing in English in Berlin, their heavy accents, their clumsy eagerness, made the tune. By the time the Doors took it up half a century later it had aged so well it fell into their hands. Their version was better than the original, where Lenya—by 1967 most easily recalled as the hideous KGB officer Rosa Klebb in the second James Bond movie—rushed the verses, dragged back on the chorus. When she sang it after the war she smoothed out all the rough spots; the tipsy woman stumbling from doorpost to doorpost gave it that big toothpaste smile. The Doors raised up the paper moon, waved at it, kept knocking on the doors of one bar after another even though it was 4 a.m. and the bars had been dark for hours. With "The Unknown Soldier" the band remembers everybody is doing it, doing it, doing it, as Marcel Janco murmured in 1916 in Zurich in the Cabaret Voltaire, but doesn't remember how to do it.

In 1968 there were a lot of people declaring that the war was over, as the Doors would do in "The Unknown Soldier." In whispery tones that fell back before the power of his own words, Allen Ginsberg had announced "The war . . . is over now," in 1966 in his Vietnam-as-Kansas, Kansas-as-Vietnam epic, "Wichita Vortex Sutra"—only to come back minutes later in complete exasperation: "The war was over several hours ago!" *Why hasn't anybody noticed?* In 1971 John Lennon and Yoko Ono would be draping WAR IS OVER IF YOU WANT IT banners over their beds. In 1968 the Doors were trying to act it out.

On record, as a single that barely scraped the Top 40, then as a track on *Waiting for the Sun*, the band's floppy third album and their only number one LP, "The Unknown Soldier" began with faraway, echoey sound effects. Boots marched through the song from the left speaker to the right, from one side of the room to the other, from the passenger seat to the driver's seat. It ended with easily rolling, everything's-all-right riffs from Robby Krieger over the sound of cheering crowds rushing through the suddenly warless streets: the Doors' own V-V Day, unless it was Vietnam's V-USA Day. It was not stirring, except for the hokey segment in the middle: the soldiers marched, Jim Morrison called out "Present! Arms!" you heard a rifle lock and load, John Densmore played a long military drum roll, and there was a rifle shot. Loud, brittle, harsh. A quick sound, and the band went back to the song too quickly. The shot didn't hang in the air—but it was still frightening. In 1968, that sound—sudden, despite the fanfare; louder than you expected, because you could guess what was coming; louder than you were expecting, if you'd heard the record before—sudden, loud, brittle, harsh—was not a metaphor. It carried events inside of it. As you heard the sound, you saw what happened.

Neither Martin Luther King, Jr., or Robert F. Kennedy had been shot when "The Unknown Soldier" was released as a single in March, but people were already asking, incessantly, under their breath, maybe when either man appeared on the nightly news, which could be almost every night, if it would happen, and when it would happen. It had already happened, with John F. Kennedy, with Malcolm X: the most unsettling thing about the line "Dead president's corpse in the driver's car" on *Waiting for the Sun,* in the musically incoherent "Not to Touch the Earth," was that it wasn't specific, wasn't necessarily about JFK; it was an image floating over the tableau of everyday life.

The story carried by that rifle crack was happening with police and people in the streets shooting to kill in Watts, Newark, Harlem, Detroit, in race riots so fierce, so ambitious, you could feel the nation cracking. It was happening every day, thousands of times over, in Vietnam. It was happening in Germany, when the student leader Rudi Dutschke was shot; in Czechoslovakia, when the Soviet Union erased Prague Spring as if to laugh at the naïveté of French students and workers with their May days; in Mexico City, where government forces shot uncounted hundreds of protesting students, and then spent forty years keeping both the bodies and any public memory of the killings buried. But in the United States, the specter had as much power as the fact. In 1965, Phil

Ochs had fantasized that, after *Highway 61 Revisited*, a set of songs about the country rushing down its own spine as a police car turned on its siren and gave chase, Bob Dylan would not be able to get on a stage: "He's gotten inside so many people's heads—Dylan has become part of so many people's psyches—and there's so many screwed up people in America, and death is such a part of the American scene now." The declension in the phrases, the way they fade away from each other, as if they don't want to hear each other, is as musical as any song Ochs ever wrote. For many reasons, some of them not from another country than the one Ochs was describing, except for one night to gather with others to praise Woody Guthrie, Dylan did not set foot on a stage in 1968.

What the Doors didn't have to remember in 1968, as they tried to find a way to make "The Unknown Soldier" convincing, not a joke, was dread. In 1968 dread was the currency. It was what kept you up all night, and not just the night Bobby Kennedy was shot, when before his death was finally announced Norman Mailer swore he'd give up an arm if Kennedy lived; dread was what made the promise believable when Mailer wrote about it. That was because people all over the country had lived through the same long night, thought the same thoughts, made the same promises, knowing they would all come up cold.

Dread was why every day could feel like a trap. There was murder everywhere; Camus's argument, in *The Rebel*, that in the modern world every act leads to murder, came off the page both as common sense and a curse. The feeling that the country was coming apart—that, for what looked and felt like a casually genocidal war in Vietnam, the country had committed crimes so great they could not be paid, that the country deserved to live out its time in its own ruins—was so visceral that the presidential election felt like a sideshow.

In this setting, the Doors were a presence. They were a band people felt they had to see—not to learn, to find out, to hear the message, to get the truth, but to be in the presence of a group of people who appeared to accept the present moment at face value. In their whole demeanor—unsmiling, no rock 'n' roll sneer but a performance of mistrust and doubt— they didn't promise happy endings. Their best songs said happy endings weren't interesting, and they weren't deserved.

You can imagine Manzarek, Densmore, Morrison, and Krieger bagging their scheduled rehearsals and songwriting sessions for *Waiting for the Sun* and cutting into a movie theater to see *Wild in the Streets*, the AIP youth-revolt exploitation number staring Christopher Jones as the rock 'n' roll singer and president of the United States Max Frost, Shelley Winters as Frost's mother, Larry "The Hook" Bishop and Richard "Stanley X" Pryor as Frost's compatriots, and Hal Holbrook, Ed Begley, and a completely numb Diane Varsi as U.S. senators—not to mention, around the edges of the frame, Dick Clark, Peter Tork, Gary Busey, Melvin Belli, Bobby Sherman, and Walter Winchell—and the Doors in their seats saying, *Hey, that's us! This is just "Five to One" with movie stars!*

More than forty years later, "Five to One," the band's own youth-revolt exploitation number from *Waiting for the Sun*, was still probably getting more airplay than anything else on the album, even more than "Hello, I Love You," which three years before, when Manzarek, Morrison, Densmore, and Manzarek's brothers Rick and Jim recorded a demo version, was not the embarrassment it would become in 1968.* "We're takin' over," Morrison slurred, sounding as if revolution was about as interesting as a bunch of bikers taking over a bar. *Wild in the Streets* was more interesting: a corrupt senator jumps on the youth bandwagon, thinking that a law lowering the voting age to fourteen will get him to the White House— when instead it's Max Frost who takes over, and sends every-one over thirty to reeducation camps where they're fed LSD all day long. Christopher Jones was the latest in the long line of new James Deans, but with his soft, shapely features, he was also the first new Jim Morrison. The match was impossible to miss; that might have been precisely why he was cast. And while as discourse on revolt *Wild in the Streets* trumped "Five to One" many times over, the revolt the Doors momentarily embodied, and acted out, was not only a matter of bad lyrics and cartoon music, which is all "Five to One" is. *Bullshit!* you can hear the Doors crowing in the theater. *If that turkey makes*

---

*"One night at TT&G studios in Hollywood, where we were recording at $100 an hour, Paul Rothchild took us by the hands and dragged us from the control room into the studio for one of his little talks. He said that we needed a hit soon and that 'Hello, I Love You,' with a tight arrangement, could fit the bill," John Densmore wrote twenty-two years later. "It turned into an unusual song with tons of distortion on the guitar via the latest elec-tronic toy, the fuzz box. Robby had also suggested a catchy way of turning the beat around à la Cream's 'Sunshine of Your Love.' Though I liked the lyrics very much, the new arrangement seemed contrived. When it climbed to number one, I was baffled." A song about a real situation that has some tiny drama in it—someone going up to someone else on the street and shamelessly saying what he feels—is made into something stupid, ob-noxious, a rock star preening, by a jerky arrangement that leaves everyone sounding phony.

it to the White House with that "Soul Kitchen" rip-off—what's it called?

"Shape of Things to Come."

Then Jim wins in a walk! And if Diane Varsi can stand up there in the Senate banging her tambourine instead of giving a speech, Ray's already secretary of state!

As an actor, and in his life offstage—sometimes barely off-stage, as with his backstage encounter with a cop at a show in New Haven in 1967, which led to Morrison being arrested *on* stage—Jim Morrison didn't really challenge authority. Rather he conveyed an unlimited, instinctive, but dramatized contempt for authority—which is to say a contempt that was thought through, theorized, a stance footnoted with mental references to Artaud and *Un Chien Andalou.*

"Morrison was one of the few if not the only performer I knew who really believed what he was saying," Robby Krieger said in 2006.

He wasn't just up there doing his trip and then he'd go home and have a beer and laugh at it all, laugh all the way to the bank. He was a guy that, he lived that life that he lived out onstage all the time. And when he went home it was just some cheap motel somewhere, and he just hung out until the next show, you know. Sometimes he would be the greatest guy you'd ever want to meet—super polite, together, clean, and everything else—but the next day he'd be completely the other way. All those stories are true, most of them: He lived his whole life right on the edge, and people could sense that when he was onstage; there was always something under there, ready to happen—and if they were lucky that night, it might happen. All I can say is that he was totally committed to living the life of the revolution.

Some of that is there in "The Unknown Soldier" as the Doors performed it in Denmark on September 18, 1968. Here the slowness of the music—the way its parts are fitted together, the deliberateness of the pacing, which suggests people feeling their way through a situation with all the lights off—produces not suspense but a sense of inevitability. Ray Manzarek gets up from the organ and walks behind John Densmore, seemingly to adjust an amplifier, then stands waiting with his head bowed as Densmore plays his roll. Manzarek lifts the amplifier, getting ready to drop it. Robby Krieger lifts his guitar and aims the neck like the barrel of a rifle, lowers it slightly, raises it again, his posture like that of an executioner, his eyes like those of a psychopath. Morrison stands waiting—for what? In the little play of the ensemble, were they performing a deserter's execution, a death in combat, a suicide? That Morrison so fully communicates with his body and the tilt of his head that he has seen this coming makes the shot Krieger fires, backed by the sound of the amplifier hitting the floor, that much more shocking: as you watch the video of the performance, you are sucked into Morrison's mind so fully you might forget anyone else is there, that anything is about to happen. "A Doors concert," Morrison said in 1968, "is a public meeting called by us for a special kind of dramatic discussion." "I'd like to play in a club where we could be with other people," he told a *Chicago Tribune* writer after a show in New York the year before. "Maybe we wouldn't even play. It would be great to sit down and talk with the audience, to get rid of all the separate tables and have one big table."

In Denmark, Morrison goes down out of the frame as if he's been erased from it—but in that instant it is the sound of the shot that throws everything off. It's not a crack, a report, an explosion. It's a long, acrid scratch; it sounds as if Krieger is scraping the inside of his strings with his fingernails. It's not a sound you've heard before, or want to hear again. It was the sound of the times that no one else made.

John Densmore, *Riders on the Storm: My Life with Jim Morrison and the Doors* (New York: Delacorte, 1990), 85, 160. This relentlessly questioning memoir is the best book on the Doors: filled with detail, powered by a sense of unreality, self-deprecating, funny, with Densmore emerging as no hero, no so-called survivor, but, as his title implies, someone along for the ride, on the storm of the times, on the storm he and the rest of the band made themselves.

Jim Morrison, quoted from Jerry Hopkins, "The Rolling Stone Interview," *Rolling Stone*, July 26, 1969. Collected in *The Rolling Stone Interviews* (New York: Paperback Library, 1971), 229–30. Probably the best single interview with Morrison; Hopkins was a trusted chronicler. The book referenced is long out of print and as a pocket book not likely collected by libraries, but the interview is greatly abridged in the more accessible *The Rolling Stone Interviews*, ed. Jann S. Wenner and Joe Levy (New York: Back Bay, 2007).

"Alabama Song (Whisky Bar)," *The Doors* (Elektra, 1967). The Kurt Weill–Bertolt Brecht collaboration premiered in *Mahogany*.

"The Unknown Soldier" and "Five to One," *Waiting for the Sun* (Elektra, released July 1968). The 2006 reissue includes a DVD with footage of the Denmark performance.

Phil Ochs, interview in Broadside (1965). Quoted in Clinton
Heylin, *Behind the Shades* (New York: Viking, 1991).

Wild in the Streets, directed by
Barry Shear, written by Robert
Thom (American International
Pictures, 1968).

Max Frost and the Troopers,
"Shape of Things to Come"
(Tower, 1968).

Robby Krieger, in *The Doors with
Ben Fong-Torres, The Doors*
(New York: Hyperion, 2006),
107.

Jim Morrison, quoted in Michael
Lydon, "The Doors: Can They
Still 'Light My Fire'?" *New
York Times,* January 19, 1969.

———, "The New Generation:
Theater with a Beat," from the *Chicago Tribune,* carried in the
San Francisco Chronicle, September 28, 1967.

Strange Days

R AY MANZAREK'S OPENING into "Strange Days" makes the spookiest moment in the Doors' career, and one of the most alluring. It's been lost; the rest of the song swallows it up. It was lost almost from the moment it appeared. Today it can pull itself out of the rest of the music, and you can play it all day long.

It was the first track and the title song of their second album, released nine months after the first, which was anything but unusual in 1967—in 1965 and 1966, Bob Dylan put out *Bringing It All Back Home, Highway 61 Revisited,* and *Blonde on Blonde* in little more than a year. But the Doors' first album had a number one single, and even though the charts stopped the album itself at #2, in the real world it was probably number one anyway. The second album—whatever it was going to be, whatever it was going to be called, whatever its cover would be, in this case a circus strongman, a man playing a horn, a mime, a juggler, and a dwarf, all in all an image of strangeness so obviously self-referential it all but put the album title in scare quotes, a tableau so corny you can almost read the casting call, a picture that immediately sent one message to fans, "Uh-oh"—had to match the first, in drama, in reach, in glamour. And in strangeness. That was the band's appeal; that was their shtick; that was their theme; that was what they had to say, or they had nothing to say. "Strange Days," *Strange Days*: they were putting their cards on the table.

Doot do
Doot do

Doot do
Doot do

Doot do
Doot do

Doot do
Doot do

Eight notes in four pairs, beginning high, with the trebly sound so common in Los Angeles record studios in the mid-1960s, but cleaner, clearer, the sound like its own tunnel through the night the sound itself was calling up. Eight notes chasing each other in four pairs, the theme repeating four times in seven unrushed seconds, a pace that was menacing, threatening, in its first split-second, calming, reassuring, halfway through—*You've been here before, you're still here, whatever this place is, it'll be here when you get back.* It was a little panorama of dream, fright, and, really, mission: to get to the other side of these strange days. A bet that there was another side.

Each eight-note pattern was lifted higher than the one before it. It was a lilting, lyrical staircase made all of spotlights, each light going dark as soon as one pair passed the baton to the pair ahead of it on the way to the end of the phrase. The race only felt as if it were in slow motion. In truth the pace was quick, nimble, with leaps over the gaps between sounds; it was the shapeliness of the design, an order that the listener was instantly sucked into, that seemed to organize the world, that made the drama of the four pairs of eight notes repeated four times in seven seconds feel distant, receding as it pulled you toward it. In 1967, those notes would have made people think of *The Twilight Zone*, even as they detached the show, a derelict caboose on a runaway train, from the history the notes were already reaching for; today it can feel as if the song was reaching for David Lynch's *Lost Highway*, reaching right through it.

There's a flipped bass thump—for the Doors' first album, and on stage, Manzarek used a bass piano device to compensate for the lack of an actual person in the band playing bass; for their second album, they brought in Douglas Lubahn of the short-lived Elektra band and Doors imitators Clear Light—then a doomy strum from Robby Krieger. Manzarek's theme moves from one channel to the other, but it's no longer the voice of the song, just a sound effect, losing its shape, as the song goes on turning into trash, the psychedelic junk you could find in any doorway on Sunset Strip. Jim Morrison comes in, and within less than a minute you could be listening to "I Had Too Much to Dream (Last Night)," the 1966 hit by the San Fernando Valley band the Electric Prunes, a group that had originally called themselves Jim and the Lords, which effortlessly translates into a name a forty-five-year-old Morrison, having no right to "The Doors" after the original group broke up in 1973, might along with a few cultist back-ups have been toting around the same Valley clubs the original Jim and the Lords briefly escaped. Everything clean, direct, straight, unblinking, and fearless in the song is gone, buried under thick, ham-handed, pumped-up breaks between one side of the song and another. The pattern set in those first seconds leads into a melody that Morrison can't sing, that stretches his voice into an ugly, convoluted tangle, and the suspended, transparent tone of "The Crystal Ship," Morrison's version of Manzarek's seven seconds, is broken into whines and wheezes. At two minutes, the music seems to have been playing for six.

At first, what Morrison was singing matched the black hole Manzarek had opened up: "Strange days have tracked us down." You could go anywhere with an idea like that, but if you were a singer, if you were a band, you needed music to get you there, to shape that idea into a sound that would arrive in the world as if it had always been there, and leave it different than it had been before it arrived: for "Strange Days," a world that was harder, more desperate, more exciting, the stakes raised. "There are songs that are ideas, and songs that are records," Phil Spector was saying as the Doors were recording "Strange Days"—after his production of Ike and Tina Turner's "River Deep, Mountain High" failed to come anywhere near the Top 40, let alone reach number one, where Spector knew it belonged, he locked up his studio and began lecturing at colleges—and, he said with characteristic modesty, "Whoever can create a song that is both an idea and a record can rule the world." It was unclear if rule the world meant top the charts or *rule the world*—that's why it was scary to hear him say it, even as you tried to understand what he meant. "Da Doo Ron Ron" might have been it, Spector mused from the stage in his pompadour, his tight suit, his ruffled cuffs, his elevator heels, his eyes flashing with intelligence and mistrust.

For seven seconds, the Doors were almost there. That was closer than most people ever got. As Al Kooper wrote in 1968 in a review of the Band's first album, *Music from Big Pink*, "There are people who will work their lives away in vain and not touch it."

"Strange Days," *Strange Days* (Elektra, 1967).

Electric Prunes, "I Had Too Much to Dream (Last Night)" (Reprise, 1966, #11). In 1972 Lenny Kaye made it the lead track of his wildly influential historical compilation *Nuggets: Original Artyfacts from the First Psychedelic Era, 1965–1968* (Elektra).

Ike and Tina Turner, "River Deep, Mountain High" (Philles, 1966, #88).

Al Kooper, review of the Band, "Music from Big Pink," *Rolling Stone*, August 10, 1968.

People Are Strange

Unlike "STRANGE DAYS," which was a theme song, a manifesto, "People Are Strange" was just a song — the Doors had been carrying it around since 1966 before it appeared as a single in September 1967. It was a small song, kin to "Alabama Song," with a loose, flapping honky-tonk piano giving it a sound halfway between the circus in the U.S.A. in the 1950s and a cabaret in Berlin in 1929. It stopped at #12.

Was Jim Morrison too good looking, more a swagger on two feet than a person, to feel as strange as the person in this song? Eve Babitz didn't think so. Having propositioned him at the London Fog in early 1966, she looked back in 1991, as part of the media orchestration for *The Doors* — one of scores of Is-Oliver-Stone's-Jim-Morrison-the-*real* Jim-Morrison? pieces. "Val Kilmer is supposed to have gotten Jim's looks exactly right," Babitz wrote, "but what can Val Kilmer know of having been fat all of his life and suddenly one summer taking so much LSD and waking up a prince? Val Kilmer has always been a prince, so he can't have the glow." Jim Morrison wasn't cool, she said: "It was so corny naming yourself after something Aldous Huxley wrote. I mean, The Doors of Perception . . . what an Ojaigeeky-too-L.A.-pottery-glazer kind of uncool idea." His girlfriend Pamela Courson, Babitz said, "was the cool one . . . She had guns, took heroin, and was fearless in every situation . . . Whereas all he had previously brought to the moment was morbid romantic excess, he now had someone looking at him and saying, 'Well, are you going to drive off this cliff, or what?'"

Listening to "People Are Strange," it isn't hard to believe the singer knows what he's talking about. Robby Krieger's guitar smoothly, confidently, walks Morrison into the tune, and some of that confidence stays with him, until the last word of the first verse. "Faces look ugly, when you're alone" slips by, sung so lightly it's like a firefly, but that lightness is gone two lines later. "Streets are uneven, when you're down"—the *down* almost cut off, running into a wall, face first, the words squeezed shut: *down*. It's such a displacing effect—or not an effect at all, but an action, a tiny event inside a rehearsed, arranged, constructed performance—it can hide the strangeness, the truth, of the line itself: someone so out of joint the streets he or she walks are thrown out of joint. Someone else can walk down the same streets a minute later and not notice that anything is wrong.

The next time the line comes up in the song, the *down* sealing the moment, deliciously, unwinding like kite string, the word no longer remotely means what it says; the song has taken it all back. By the end it's a happy sing-along. So that first *down* sticks, thuds, echoes.

So often, the Doors lost their songs as the songs took shape. Did they pull back? Did Paul Rothchild polish the music until the shine was unbreakable and the glow as evanescent as, really, a glow has to be? At the end of the 2006 reissue of *Strange Days*, there were extra tracks; one was of a few false starts for "People Are Strange." "Gentlemen, new sensations the Doors make another album," Rothchild says from the control booth. "Here we go, this is going to be take three, a multiple of, you know, divisible of *six*, nine, and all those other magic numbers, take three." There's a long pause. Krieger tunes with a strum, then the outline of a riff; there's a squeak from the organ. There's more talk; again, "Take three." And then there is the warmest, most suggestive drawn-out circle of a roll fingered on the strings—a figure suggestive not only of emotions yet to be felt, words yet to be spoken, songs yet to be played, but lives yet to be lived—suggestive most of all of an opening into a bigger story than the song as it was recorded, the first time, the third time, the twenty-fourth time, ever meant to tell. "Okay, pick it up from right there," Rothchild says. "Not pick it up, start it again, that was really groovy. Twenty-five—" Krieger plays a couple of dead notes. "Gentlemen, that could be our take, lets do another one, right now. Go right into it, here we go, twenty-eight, nine?" "Uh, seven," someone says. "Twenty-seven," Rothchild announces. Krieger steps in again, his sound lower, louder, bigger, but the story in the notes smaller.

"People Are Strange," *Strange Days* (Elektra, 1967). "People Are Strange (False Starts & Studio Dialogue)," *Strange Days* (Elektra/Rhino, 2006).

Eve Babitz, "Jim Morrison Is Alive and Well and Living in Hollywood," *Esquire*, March 1991. A portrait in cool—the author's—that keeps breaking down, and probably worth more than all the Doors memoirs save John Densmore's. With a drawing of Morrison as he would have looked twenty years after: pudgy, dull-eyed, not as cool as the reader.

My Eyes Have Seen You

Another staircase: Tenochtitlán, to the top, in a sprint, then looking down as the fireworks begin.

"My Eyes Have Seen You," *Strange Days* (Elektra, 1967).

Twentieth Century Fox

O N *The Doors*, "Twentieth Century Fox" was less a song than a Lichtenstein: pop art. It had that pop sheen, the irony, the sardonic grin: *You don't think I'm fooled, do you?* Unlike Rolling Stones songs about women who needed to be put in their place — "Under My Thumb," which you can almost see the singer rehearsing in a mirror, or the dizzying "Miss Amanda Jones" — the Doors' portrait of the perfect L.A. woman was all bright colors, full of affection, even envy. Guys had it tough. They had to go out and race Dead Man's Curve, shoot the curl, score dope, pay for dinner, and stand up in front of people and be famous. If they could pull it off, all girls had to do was strut, and with the band's jerky, high-heels beat behind her, this one could pull it off. She didn't look forward, she didn't look back. She let the looks come to her; she saw the world through everyone else's eyes, as if looks shot right through her and gave her X-ray vision. Banking off the keyed drums-organ-guitar crunches of the sound, Jim Morrison's vocal was all highs and lows, nothing in between, the stuttering breaks of the tune in step with "Alabama Song" and "People Are Strange." If "Light My Fire" hadn't made the Doors into stars you can hear how their music could have curdled into artiness, everything self-referential, post-modern, each note a parody of something else, not a word needing to mean what it said, the group more popular in Paris or Milan, especially during fashion week, than anywhere in America, just like Chet Baker. In this world, "Twentieth Century Fox" was never a hit—neither was anything else—but after a few years it was the song everyone wanted to hear.

| | |

IN THE SPRING OF 2001 I was in Paris, at the Pompidou Center, walking through *Les années pop*, a huge show of pop art from 1956 to 1968. On the walls were most of the usual masterpieces, all the big names, plus much more. Architecture: numerous plans for the sort of utopian houses and cities no one would ever want to live in. Tupperware. Movies: film of Andy Warhol's Exploding Plastic Inevitable, and Bruce Conner's *A Movie*, his hilarious collage film of disaster footage. Artifacts: album covers, Richard Avedon's *Life* magazine Beatle portraits. Clothes. Posters. Newsreels. Music playing in all the galleries.

The museum was packed. Pop art shows are always popular, because pop art is easy to relate to. It's big, it's glamorous, and it's full of references everyone knows, that leave no one out. But almost everything seemed beside the point. I wasn't sure what point—it was just . . . pointlessness. The music playing was the same. If there was a true spirit of pop art, it wasn't in Elvis Presley's "Heartbreak Hotel," the Marvelettes' "Please Mr. Postman," Jefferson Airplane's "Somebody to Love"—though it was, somehow, present in the Tornadoes' 1962 "Telstar," that weird piece of British surf music celebrating the first telecommunications satellite. With the organ sounding like a bagpipe—the sound was so tinny, distant, and distorted you could imagine it really was the first thing bounced off Telstar—the record was cheap, corny, and triumphant: irresistible. It sounded right. "Twentieth Century Fox" would have been almost too right. "Light My Fire" or "Take It as It Comes" would have blown down the conceptual walls that were holding up the whole show.

I began thinking that there was a lot less here than met the eye. Why was there so little art that seemed to live up to its name, and so little music that lived up to that art? It was as if pop culture, something real, had been hijacked by pop art— by something that wasn't real.

Once, trying to figure out what pop culture was, I ended up with the phrase "the folk culture of the modern market." Pop culture is a culture in which people tell themselves, and tell each other, stories about the modern market. That doesn't mean the billboard Elektra Records put up over Sunset Strip to announce the Doors' first album, a marketing first; it means an unknown station playing unknown music, until both turn into secrets everyone wants to tell. The modern market is a field of rumors and tall tales, promises and threats, warnings and prophecies: as people talk, pop culture is landscape and the change of seasons, war and peace, the clearing of forests and the building of cities, religious revivals and moral panics, wealth and poverty, adventure and discovery, sex and death, citizenship and exile.

You can hear this in the way *The Doors* went from an L.A. scenester's secret to all-American password, and you can see it in two founding works of pop culture: Eduardo Paolozzi's 1947 collage *I Was a Rich Man's Plaything* and Chuck Berry's 1955 "No Money Down." Paolozzi was the most playful, aesthetically omnivorous member of England's Independent Group—the small post-war combine of architects, visual artists, and critics who were drawn to the commercial imagery of American culture, who could not see themselves in what Independent Group member Richard Hamilton called "hard-edged American painting," abstract expressionism, Jackson Pollock, the new art everyone was supposed to be thrilled by. With rationing still a fact of daily life in Britain, the Independent Group was eager to get out of the war, out of the post-war, into a new real life.

As an artist, Paolozzi was already living it. "Wherever he went," his Independent Group comrade Lawrence Alloway remembered, "he was, you know, bending things, drawing things, turning paper plates into something, so that he was habitually an improvising working artist . . . he was kind of someone who had this itchy creativity on a continuous basis, always being bombarded by mass-media imagery."

The glee, the promiscuousness with which Paolozzi scavenged for his images—images taken from women's magazines, advertisements, comic books—tells you it might be closer to the mark to say he was always exposing himself to mass media imagery. It might be closer than that to say Paolozzi was swimming in it—like Carl Barks's Uncle Scrooge, swimming through oceans of coins in his money bin. Like the Berlin dada collage artist Hannah Höch, swimming through the imagery of her own post-war, in the 1920s, criticizing the subjugation of women, satirizing gender roles, and also reveling in fashion and style, shoes and makeup.

Walter Benjamin spoke of "art in the age of mechanical reproduction"; what you can see in Paolozzi's work is the thrill of mechanical reproduction. At the center of *I Was a Rich Man's Plaything* is the cover of an issue of *Intimate Confessions*, with a smiling woman in a skimpy red dress and black stockings, her legs drawn up to her chest. Pasted in is a man's hand holding a big, ugly, fearsome-looking handgun to the head of the rich man's plaything—unless she is, as described on the right side of the magazine cover, the "Ex-Mistress," the "Woman of the Streets," or the "Daughter of Sin," or unless they're all the same person. Out of the barrel of the gun comes a cloud of smoke and the word "POP!" There's cherry pie and Coca-Cola and the logo "Real Gold" and a fighter plane.

"I think we were actually fundamentally anti-pop," the architect Peter Smithson of the Independent Group said in 1976. "That is," he said, "the interest in current phenomena, current imagery—imagery that was thrown up by production, by advertising and so on, that was studied by the Independent Group—each person in the group was studying it for his own reasons. One emerges from it as one went into it, with more information, with one's lines established. But certainly, those who used the information directly—isn't that a handsome picture or a handsome layout which I could parody for a fine art picture?—I really think that is a completely meaningless activity."

It's no fun to read this argument today—"one emerges from it" as if from a swamp, from the modern market in which people actually live, "as one went into it," confirmed in one's conviction that one cannot be changed by the market, that one is immune to it, superior to it. "One's lines" are "established"—that is, one's distance from the world in which people actually live is plotted on a map.

But you don't feel any of this coming out of Paolozzi's work. You feel that thrill of mechanical reproduction—the collage maker, the person who saw *Intimate Confessions* on the newsstand and said, *I have to have that,* who then brought it home and said, *Now, what am I going to do with this?*

This is someone who liked to argue with what wasn't yet called pop culture—the cheap, fast sounds and images that in the years immediately after the Second World War seemed to be coming together everywhere, the sounds and images connecting to each other in ways that seemed at once natural and inexplicable, the artifacts of this emerging folk culture of the modern market speaking in code, speaking a secret language. Cutting and pasting, Paolozzi is someone who is trying to learn that language and speak it himself. You can sense someone saying, *This stuff is out there, everyone is seeing it, everyone is responding to it, I am responding to it. I'm turned on by the woman on the cover of this month's* Intimate Confessions, *but I'll bet someone else is much more excited by a Coca-Cola bottle—and not in a different way. I've got to do something with my reaction—I've got to make it into my own language. I've got to tell people about this. I've got to make this into something so*

I don't forget it—not the magazine, I can keep that, but the feel-ing I had when I saw it on the newsstand this morning.

"I don't make the mistake that high culture mongers do of assuming that because people like cheap art, their feelings are cheap, too," the late filmmaker Dennis Potter once said, ex-plaining why pop songs were so important in his work, from *Pennies from Heaven* to *The Singing Detective* to *Lipstick on Your Collar*, his paean to the 1950s, the time he shared with the Independent Group—and Potter was also defining a pop ethos, defining what I think is happening in Paolozzi's collage.

"When people say, 'Oh, listen, they're playing our song,'" Potter said, "they don't mean, 'Our song, this little cheap, tin-kling, syncopated piece of rubbish is what we felt when we met.' What they're saying is, 'That song reminds me of the tremendous feeling we had when we met.' Some of the songs I use are great anyway, but the cheaper songs are still in the di-rect line of descent from David's Psalms. They're saying, 'Lis-ten, the world isn't quite like this, the world is better than this, there is love in it,' 'There's you and me in it,' or 'The sun is shining in it.' So-called dumb people, simple people, unedu-cated people, have as authentic and profound depth of feeling as the most educated on earth. And anyone who says different is a fascist."

Chuck Berry's "No Money Down" is as much a fantasy, a montage of advertisements and commercial slogans, as *I Was a Rich Man's Plaything*. It was a follow-up to Berry's first hit, the 1955 "Maybellene." In that first song the singer is chasing Maybellene's Cadillac in his beat-up Ford—he catches her, but the chase draws the Ford's last breath. So now he's down at the dealer's, buying his own Cadillac. The use of a melodra-matic, stop-time beat later used for the theme of the *Pink*

Panther movies, with Peter Sellers as Inspector Clouseau—da dadada *da* da . . . da . . .—lets Berry open the story in the slyest, most confiding voice, as if a crime is about to be committed. *This is a great story*, he's whispering. *This is* much *too good to tell out loud. You won't* believe *what I got away with.*

The car salesman tells Berry he can have whatever he wants—in an hour. Berry starts off demanding a yellow convertible. He wants a big motor—with "jet off-take." The salesman doesn't blink; Berry doesn't slow down. In fact he picks up the pace, and now you can see everyone in the bar, on the street, wherever it is that he's telling this story, gathering around to hear what happens next, what's at stake, who wins, who loses. Now the storyteller is practically a preacher, offering salvation: what it is—how to get it.

I told the car dealer, Berry says, that I wanted a complete fold-out bed in my back seat—and before he could get a word out I told him what else I wanted. It was 1955, but I could see the future, and I wasn't going to wait: short-wave radio, a telephone and a television. He looked like his hair was going to catch fire, but he said yes, and I didn't stop. Four carburetors, straight exhaust—I said, "I'm burning aviation fuel, no matter what the cost." Air horns. A spotlight that would scatter crowds like cockroaches. He was turning green when we sat down in the office, and I wrote it down: five-year guarantee. I made his head spin with deductibles, notes, liability, and then I pulled the ace: no money down. Anything, he said. He blinked twice and gave me the pen. I put down my John Hancock; he wrote John Smith.

If Eduardo Paolozzi and Chuck Berry aren't speaking exactly the same language, though they probably are, they can certainly talk to each other, each telling the other stories he'd want to hear, and pass on. But the kind of apology, explanation, and rescue job one has to perform on Paolozzi—rescuing him from the doubts and fears of those around him—would be completely meaningless with "No Money Down."

It would be ridiculous. In terms of detail, layering, recoloring, collage, glamour, and speed, with "No Money Down"— or Berry's "You Can't Catch Me" or "No Particular Place to Go," or for that matter K. C. Douglas's "Mercury Blues," or the Beach Boys' "409" or "Fun, Fun, Fun"—there's no apparent distance at all.

Whatever distance or irony there might have been in anyone's intention—Chuck Berry's, K. C. Douglas's, Brian Wilson's—is long gone before the song ever gets out into the world, to the public, into the market, where people will start talking about it. After all, in the terms of the market, car songs are part car, and cars are part car songs. You hear them in the car.

Peter Smithson's questions of aesthetics—his speaking of establishing one's lines, of "isn't that a handsome picture or a handsome layout which I could parody for a fine art picture"—are really questions of ethics: how one remains clean. Such a question can hardly come up in pop music, which when it began, in the 1950s, was not only part car. With payola—with small, regional, independent record labels like Berry's Chess in Chicago or the Penguins' Dootone in Los Angeles paying disc jockeys to play their records, the only way they could get their records on a radio dominated by huge New York corporations like Columbia and RCA—with bribery, lies, manipulation, and even extortion, pop music was part used car salesman. But there are all kinds of salesmen.

In 1990, the late Kirk Varnedoe, then curator of painting and sculpture at the Museum of Modern Art in New York, published a book called *A Fine Disregard: What Makes Modern Art Modern*. The title—and the theory it spoke for—came from a stone marker that stands at the gates of the Rugby School in England, one of the most elite, exclusive, and aristocratic schools in the world. Varnedoe rests all of modern art on this stone, which commemorates the exploits of one William Ellis Webb, who, in 1823, "with" the stone says, "a fine disregard for the rules of football as played in his time, first took the ball in his arms and ran with it, thus originating the distinctive feature of the rugby game."

It seems to me that the determinant word here is less disregard—for rules, expectations, and so on—than fine. That is, we are being reassured that modern art remains art—and we are being reassured that it remains the province of the sort of people who for centuries have attended the Rugby School, or who sit on the boards of art museums. We are being told modern art will not go too far—say disregard without a modifier, after all, and you have no idea what kind of riffraff you might have to let in next.

We are being told that we can keep one sort of art here and another sort of art over there, based on class, intent, and attitude—the class, intent, and attitude of the audience as well as the artist. A fine disregard—art remains the province of those fine enough to appreciate it on the terms on which it should be appreciated, not to mention those in a position to disregard the rules, as opposed to those who aren't.

It's because of this idea of what art is, and what it is for—and I am singling out Kirk Varnedoe only because he gave such a precise voice to what is, in fact, a vast chorus—that there is, I think, really very little true pop visual art. There's very little that actually tells stories of and in the modern market, that does not keep its distance: its distance from the images it seizes, its distance from the noise it seeks to replicate, its distance from the speed, flash, and glamour it wishes to capture and contain—its distance from itself.

The 1990 show *High and Low*, curated by Varnedoe and Adam Gopnik at the Museum of Modern Art in New York, exhibited works of pop art alongside their "handsome picture or a handsome layout which I could parody for a fine art picture" sources. I was curious to go, because I had never understood why George Herriman's *Krazy Kat* comic strips, or *Steve Canyon* and *True Romance* comic books, were lesser art—or, rather, why they were not greater art—than the pop art classics Philip Guston and Roy Lichtenstein had made of them.

Displayed together, there was one undeniable difference: the Guston and Lichtenstein pictures were bigger. I remembered the late San Francisco painter, filmmaker, and assemblage artist Bruce Conner once saying he had to leave New York because he liked to work on what he called real scale—and because of the cost of living in New York when he left in the 1950s, Conner said, he would have had to work on Roy Lichtenstein scale. Here it was.

I looked at the huge pictures, still baffled. What was added, or for that matter taken away? Where was the critical vision—or any vision, beyond that of the original artists? There's no equivalent in Lichtenstein's remakes of *Steve Canyon* and *True Romance* panels to what members of the Situationist International were doing with them in Paris at the same time.

The Situationist International was a tiny, revolutionary circle of critics, so extreme they celebrated the 1965 Watts riots as "a critique of urban planning." They had a sense of humor. They photocopied favorite comics panels and put new words in the speech balloons, thus forcing square-jawed Steve and teary Priscilla to speak of alienation and the Paris Commune as if people actually cared about such things. By contrast, what Lichtenstein offered was not rewriting but, in that word utterly loaded with elitism, privilege, entitlement—with droit du seigneur—appropriation. The artist is saying, *I myself have found this image strangely appealing, powerful, odd, perverse, charming, amusing. Now I'll translate it—or, really give it voice, let it speak to the audience that matters, because on its own terms, and our terms, it is mute. I will give it the imprimatur of art—otherwise, it will pass as if it had never been.* You can imagine the Doors a few years down the line, a year or two after being dropped by their label, singing "Twentieth Century Fox," or even "Break on Through (To the Other Side)" in just this way: *We always knew there wasn't any other side—we wrote this song with a raised eyebrow at people who thought there was!*

This is not pop art—art that wants to, that can, that does tell stories about the modern market of which it is a part, or that, in whatever manner, it wishes to join—and it's not art that can really hear the stories the market is telling. This art—like Robert Rauschenberg's collages, the lifeless *Retroactive 1*, from 1964, with John F. Kennedy pointing a finger at the center and an astronaut in the top left corner, though even Rauschenberg's much better work, such as the 1963 *Kite*, is not really different, or James Rosenquist's collage murals, such as his 1960–61 *President Elect*, unless it was 1964, which is even more cynical, even more a matter of an artist superior to the subject: Kennedy smile, chocolate cake, Chevrolet—is all distance.

You can see, and feel, this distance dissolve when what's before you is a kind of frenzy of recombination, of translation, of an artist diving all the way into his or her material, certain there is a secret in the noise and speed and promises of postwar life, certain that the artist can find the secret and make it into a story anyone can understand.

A few—not many—did their work here. As opposed to Rauschenberg's this-stuff-in-our-cultural-atmosphere-is-sort-of-weird-to-me-it-ought-to-be-sort-of-weird-to-you, Richard Hamilton's unmatched House Beautiful collage—his famous *Just What Is It That Makes Today's Homes So Different, So Appealing?*—which is a much better way of asking the question "What makes modern art modern?"—is almost real life. You can't look at this and just get it, mentally write it up, which is to say write it off: establish your own distance from it.

In 1956, the year Hamilton made his collage, my family moved into a new, modest, but absolutely modern house in Menlo Park, California, just down from San Francisco. It was an Eichler house, built on the model of Rudolf Schindler's experimental Kings Road House, which the Austrian modernist constructed in West Hollywood in 1922 and occupied until his death in 1953.

The Schindler-Eichler designs were all flat planes and flat roofs, sliding glass doors instead of ordinary external walls, rooms open to the outside and to each other rather than protected, segmented areas drawing lines between construction and nature, between kitchen and conversation. Whether built as a single work of art after the First World War by Schindler or mass-produced after the Second World War by Eichler, these were utopian houses. They were designed to affirm a connection between the people in the houses and the world in which they lived, and to bring the people who lived in the houses closer to each other.

If I'd seen Richard Hamilton's *Just What Is It That Makes Today's Homes So Different, So Appealing?* in 1956, when we crossed the threshold of our piece of modernism, I would have been scared to death—as scared, and as thrilled, as I was when, in the same house, at the same time, I first heard Elvis Presley and Little Richard.

Just What Is It—in the picture you see the ancestor portrait on the wall next to the gigantic, framed *Young Romance* comic book cover, the nearly naked Charles Atlas muscleman and the even more naked wife with a party-animal lampshade on her head and one hand cupped under her huge, tinfoil-nippled, torpedo-shaped left breast. You see the Ford logo, the movie playing just outside the enormous picture window—Al Jolson's *The Jazz Singer*, as if a harbinger of the blackface pop that culture would wear across the coming decade. You see the tape recorder running on the floor, the TV on, the Hormel ham displayed as an art object on the coffee table, which actually has coffee on it—when I look at the picture today I think I can see what I would have seen in 1956, but wouldn't have been able to put into words.

I see a world where everything is of equal value, but where everything is valuable: where, therefore, cultural distinctions are meaningless, and impossible to make even if they are meaningful.

I see sexual anarchy: precisely the sort of suburban sexual anarchy—from *Playboy* to wife-swapping to the 1950s epidemic of adultery and divorce—that would sell American magazines across the coming decade, until the so-called sexual revolution of the 1960s made it all seem redundant and quaint. In documentaries about the time, you can see a teenage Marianne Faithfull speak in grainy footage, from a long-forgotten British interview show; it's about 1965. "If everyone did what you seem to be advocating," an overstuffed man says to Mick Jagger's then-girlfriend, future heroin addict, and punk avenger, the harrumphing man speaking to the thin blonde girl with the angel's face and convent voice, "do you not agree that the whole structure of society would just collapse?" "Yes," she says with a gay smile, her tone summoning up a kingdom of indulgence her interrogator will never know, "wouldn't it be lovely? I think I'm really powerful. They could—they'll smash me, probably. But I want to *try*."

That was the future contained in *Just What Is It That Makes Today's Homes So Different, So Appealing?* Looking into Hamilton's picture I see a beckoning into a dangerous funhouse—not all that different from the beckoning of the witch who lures the children she eats into her oven by means of a house made of candy.

The piece is not very big: twelve inches by eighteen and a half inches. It is balanced and elegant. You can sense the fun Hamilton had making it, and you can sense his nervousness—*Have I said enough, have I said too much, is this what makes today's homes so different, so appealing, so diabolical?*

There is an unlocking going on here—the creation of a bizarre but nevertheless obvious tableau in order to get behind the mask pop culture was already placing over the face of modernism, modern living, modern life. Comparing Hamilton's collage to most of what has gone down in history as pop art is like comparing a polite cocktail party to a drunk backing you into a corner and ranting about the price of gas, his whore of a wife, and how the Jews rule the world.

You can see the same divide between the 1960s pop art ap-
propriations of comic strip characters by Andy Warhol and
Lichtenstein—their paintings of Dick Tracy and the like—
and the Dick Tracy rewrites practiced by the late San Francisco collage artist Jess. Jess's Dick Tracy is in his *Tricky Cad*
casebooks, a vast, obsessive project he pursued from 1954 to
1958 by means of the full-color front page of the Sunday *San
Francisco Chronicle* comics section. This is not appropriation.
As Jess cut up *Dick Tracy* strips every weekend, pasting pieces
of the images back in the wrong places, tricking the characters
into speaking a gibberish that was at once blank and threatening, paranoid and superrational, gibberish you can now just
barely translate, he was engaged in a wrestling match, or declaring war.

First appearing in 1931 as a call to clean up police forces
corrupted by Prohibition, by 1954 Chester Gould's *Dick Tracy*
had become the comic strip version of McCarthyism, the Red
Scare, the search for the Enemy Within—but in Jess's hands,
the great crusade to cleanse the country turns dyslexic. DICK
TRACY—the words lose their gravity, tumbling into ICK
TRA, TRICKD, DICK RACY, TICK R—titles Jess ran across
his first *Tricky Cad*. DIRAC, they go on, KID RAT, ICKY
TAR, ICKIART, TRACKY DIRT.

Only barely leaving out the real name hiding in the ana-
grams—which would have been TRICKY DICK, in the 1950s
the liberal's nickname for Red Hunter Richard Nixon—Jess
called his work "a demon-stration of the hermetic critique
lockt up in Art." He was going to provide the key, unlock the
art, expose the critique: the story "Dick Tracy" was telling in
spite of itself.

A lot was at stake. This was a time when every form of media carried the message that Your Neighbor Could Be a Communist—or a homosexual, as Jess was. With *Tricky Cad* as his foil, Jess let the hermetic critique out of its cage: he diffused suspicion throughout the whole of society. "You haven't given us a naïve answer," says a policewoman to an old woman in custody. "Lock her up, Murphy."

"As you know," says a judge to another woman, stylishly dressed except for her head, which has been replaced by what looks like an upside-down typewriter, "you've been found guilty of *jail* abandonment, and living at home!" "I *need* no baby," says the woman in the next panel, suddenly with a head again, taking her stand against everything the American 1950s demanded of her. "Take her away for one year!" says the judge, and we never see her again.

Richard Hamilton joined in this sort of obsessive creation, the nervous exhilaration of collage at its most intense—but he too fell victim to the anxiety of identification and self-affirmation, the anxiety of the dissolution of the artist into his or her material, the anxiety that kept the hands of so many other artists cleaner than his. "Is there anything," he said in 1976, remembering the question he had asked himself twenty years before, "is there any ingredient which these pop art phenomena have which is incompatible with fine art? I said, is big business incompatible with fine art? No. And I went through a long list of all the things I associated with the art of the mass media and the only element which I thought was not compatible was expendability.

". . . When Elvis Presley produced a record, you didn't get the feeling he was making it for next year, he was making it for this week and it really didn't matter very much when it sold the first four million whether the thing was ever heard again. And I thought, this is something the fine artist cannot stomach, he cannot enter the creative process of making a work of art with an understanding that it's not going to last until next year or for very much longer than that. He has to approach it with the idea that it has some qualities which are enduring."

Now, never mind the ignorance here—the blindness to the fact that as part of a tradition, Elvis Presley's reimaginings of blues and country forms implied a future as well as a past, that just as Elvis Presley's performance changed the way people looked at their culture and themselves in the present, it changed the demands people would make on the future, and changed the way they understood the past. Never mind that the Los Angeles rock 'n' roll vocal group the Medallions put out a record called "Buick '59," in 1954—because they hoped that post-dating it by five years might keep it on the radio at least that long. Never mind that the Doors saw themselves as much in the tradition of fine art—a tradition within the tradition, the stream of art maudit that carried Blake, Poe, Baudelaire, Rimbaud, Nietzsche, Jarry, Buñuel, Artaud, and Céline to their doorsteps—as in the tradition of rock 'n' roll, or that for them rock 'n' roll itself was already a tradition, as full of heroes and martyrs as any Hamilton might appeal to. What's really interesting is this: if a pop artist as complete as Richard Hamilton can talk like this, did pop art—as a form, as a school, as opposed to those places and moments where it appeared without need of a name, as with "Twentieth Century Fox," or, four years later, in a stranger, far more shifting shape, with "L.A. Woman," which is a pop art map of a city, not a person—even exist?

Pop—the sound describes what, in the hermetic critique locked up in the art, the art might have wanted to be. Pop—it's a balloon, any color you like. It makes an image, then it makes a noise, then it's gone. All that's left are shreds of rubber, modern pottery shards, junk you could, if you wanted to, paste into another picture instead of throwing it away. The joke culture has played on certified pop artists is that what they thought was transient, ephemeral, certain to disappear—comic books, 45s, LPs, advertisements—have all lasted. They are stored in expensive art books and CD boxed sets; they are immediately accessible online anywhere in the world.

They cast spells now just as they did thirty, forty, fifty, sixty years ago—and perhaps the purest, the simplest, and most complete of all pop art works are about this casting of spells. These are the untitled Verifax collages the California assemblage artist Wallace Berman made from the mid-1960s to his death in 1976: sheets of images, like sheets of stamps, sometimes twelve, sometimes dozens, each image that of a hand holding up a tiny transistor radio, sometimes five radios at a time, spread out in a crescent like a poker hand.

Every picture was that of the same hand, the same radio—but for every replicated picture there was a different image where the radio speaker should have been. You spot a nude couple; you see Charlie Watts and Mick Jagger, a key, a motorcycle, a football player, a gun and an iron cross, a Hebrew letter, a hospital bed that looks like someone just died in it, a still from a porn movie, an astronaut, leaves, a rose, a spider, Kenneth Anger as a teenage actor, a clock, an ear, Allen Ginsberg, James Brown, fancy people emerging from a restaurant, Bob Dylan, a torn concert ticket. The Doors weren't there—

Berman was not a fan*—but it didn't matter: the form Berman created included them even in their formal absence. As he worked, they were on the radio, and the kind of music they made raised Berman's hand, holding the radio, to the ear, to a friend's ear, even a passerby's, to the air. Except that, in the greater game of appropriation that is advertising, finally the Doors were there. In 2011, an iPhone/iTunes commercial showed various albums popping up on the iPhone screen. Visually it was precisely a new version of Berman's transistor, and as clear a transposition as could be: one modern moment after another, *The Freewheelin' Bob Dylan*, Justin Bieber's *My Worlds Acoustic*, PJ Harvey's *Let England Shake*, the Clash's *London Calling*, Bright Eyes' *The People's Key*, Au Revoir Simone's *Still Night, Still Light*, Hayes Carll's *KMAG YOYO*, a score more albums against a bright white background, ending, in the border of a glowing black iPhone, with a visual gong, like an anchor dropped in time, with *The Doors*.†

---

*Berman, whose face appears on the cover of the Beatles' *Sgt. Pepper's Lonely Hearts Club Band*, was a zoot-suit jazzbo from the forties; rock 'n' roll favorites (as included on a mix-tape compiled by his son, Tosh Berman, in 2007) included the Kinks' "Who'll Be the Next in Line," the Beatles' "And I Love Her," the Righteous Brothers' "You've Lost that Lovin' Feeling," the Rolling Stones' fabulous "Tell Me," Ike and Tina Turner's "River Deep, Mountain High," Love's "Little Red Book," Roxy Music's "The Bogus Man" ("I cannot count the times I have seen my father lying on the floor in our living room with Koch headphones on listening to this track," Tosh Berman wrote in his notes to the set), Syd Barrett's "Baby Lemonade," and the New York Dolls' "Trash."

†"Apple iPhone Discovers Hot New Act: The Doors," deadtreemedia.com posted on April 19, 2011.

Berman's gesture, the way the radio was held, turned the sets of pictures into an incantation—and turned every variation into a talisman. Taken together, the little pictures made a field of images, a force field; the field vibrated. It was the most casual sort of creation, made of the most ephemeral materials— the radios no longer exist, the pop culture references were supposed to be yesterday's news a week later, no one knows anymore what the photocopying trademark Verifax signifies, but the embrace of everyday culture as a lost mine, as a repository of secrets, as an open-air museum filled with clues hidden in plain sight, was absolute.

With this cheap, easy to make, infinitely copyable art, Berman did everything pop ever implied. And he caught its theory, which is really just a dare. What is certain to disappear is certain to last, the pop dare says to whoever is afraid of pop—but what *is* certain is that the standard of value, on which the presupposition that certain things were made to endure and others were made to be forgotten, will change. Don't worry about what will last, and what won't; don't flatter yourself that your intent, your commitment to the enduring, is anything but vanity. What lasts for a decade is no more than a conspiracy of taste. What lasts for a century is an accident.

In 1986 the punk artist Shawn Kerri talked about her 1980 work in Los Angeles, her handbills and posters for local punk bands like the Circle Jerks or the Germs—work that not so many years later was being included in an expensive art book. "There are a lot of my handbills that became classics in their day," she said. "Like the one with the mohawked skull breaking through the Germs' 'coat of arms'—a blue circle, either worn on a black armband or spray-painted wherever you found a flat surface. The true initiates had a cigarette burn on their left wrist, and quite a few people had it tattooed on themselves. The 'Germs Return' flier had quite an impact on people. It was done for the show they performed shortly before Darby Crash, their lead singer, killed himself with an overdose." Crash had shot up before going on stage; the idea was to die on stage, in the middle of a song. It didn't work; by the time he died the band had run out of songs and the performance was over.

"He didn't know what I was going to do," Kerri said. "He didn't tell me what he wanted—he only said, 'do a flier.' I did it, and when I showed him the art, he was strangely excited by it. It was like a pre-post-mortem. I wondered later if he liked the Death's Head motif (the skull and hairdo are undoubtedly him) because he had suicide on his mind at the time."

"I was proud as hell of my handbills," Kerri said, summing up, looking for what made her work a thing in itself, what made it art, a step back from life, a look right into it, a picture of what life would be if life could see itself as the woman looking saw it. "I'd see them all over the place. And you know, I've never gotten the same thrill out of having one of my cartoons printed in a magazine as much as seeing one of my old fliers—something I did for a gig the week before—laying in the gutter. Seeing it all mashed and dirty *thrilled* me, because that was how I was living, too. It looked exactly like my life."

Art doesn't have to imitate life to be art—certainly the Doors' music never did. But art may have to translate life, lift it up, cast it down, take it elsewhere, bring it back from the dead, pronounce the funeral oration, again and again. For a time, at the beginning and the end, no artists faced that glamorous void with more flair, curiosity, and heedlessness than a group that, with their faces on their own billboard looking down from one end of Sunset Strip, with "Twentieth Century Fox" defaced and rewrote the billboards that were already there.

"Twentieth Century Fox," *The Doors* (Elektra, 1967).

Les années pop, 1956–1968, ed. Mark Francis (Paris: Centre Pompidou, 2001).

Lawrence Alloway quoted in *The Independent Group: Postwar Britain and the Aesthetics of Plenty* (Cambridge, MA: MIT, 1990), 43.

Eduardo Paolozzi, *I Was a Rich Man's Plaything* (1947). Included in *The Independent Group*, 97. See also *The Jet Age Compendium: Paolozzi at Ambit*, ed. David Brittain (London: Four Corners Books, 2009), a collection of Paolozzi's 1967–79 contributions to the galvanic avant-garde quarterly: a chronicle of pinups and Vietnam, as if both are at war over the artist's mind, with Vietnam winning. "The strongest doors in the world are those that guard the treasures in the great banks, insurance offices, and safe deposits," Paolozzi wrote in *Ambit* 33 in 1967, tracing a theme he would return to over the years. "They are massive pieces of steel, weighing several tons, and boasting a formidable array of bolts, combination locks and placement. The sacrifice of many measures to one, also is often the wisest disposition of forces. Upon the stage, spectacular arrangement is constructed almost entirely on this principle. The greater the number of figures supporting, or wizards. One came to me not long ago with a brainstorm. At that particular time, we had among our clients a large manufacturer of chewing gum and also one of the leading makers of toothpaste. Our boy had an idea for two new products destined for the large Italian population of the States: garlic-flavored chewing gum and garlic toothpaste. After all these years, I am still wondering did we pass up a million?"

Peter Smithson quoted in *The Independent Group*, 43.

Dennis Potter quoted in Michael Sragow, "BBC Pro Shows ABC's

of Dream Writing," *San Francisco Sunday Examiner & Chronicle*, March 29, 1987.

Chuck Berry, "No Money Down" (Chess, 1955).

Kirk Varnedoe, *A Fine Disregard: What Makes Modern Art Modern* (New York: Abrams, 1990).

Marianne Faithfull quoted in *Behind the Music: Marianne Faithfull* (VH1, 1999).

Richard Hamilton, *Just What Is It That Makes Today's Homes So Different, So Appealing?* (1956). Included in *The Independent Group*, 69. See also GM, "The Vortex of Gracious Living," in *Richard Hamilton*, ed. Hal Foster (Cambridge MA: October/ MIT, 2010).

———, On expendability. See *The Independent Group*, 40. Jim Morrison had his own argument. "That's what I love about films— they're so perishable," he said in 1969. "One big atomic explosion and all the celluloid melts. There'd be no film. There's a beautiful scene in a book called *Only Lovers Left Alive* . . . this guy's making a foray into enemy territory—the kids have inherited the earth; all the adults have committed suicide—and at night he stumbles into this abandoned building and he hears a strange noise. What it is is a gang of little kids between six and twelve years old, huddled around a dead television set, and one of them is imitating the television shows of old. I think that's beautiful. And that's why poetry appeals to me so much—because it's eternal. As long as there are people, they can remember words and combinations of words. Nothing else can survive a holocaust, but poetry and songs. No one can remember an entire novel. No one can describe a film, a piece of sculpture, a painting. But so long as there are human beings, songs and poetry can continue." From Jerry Hopkins, "The Rolling Stone Interview," *Rolling Stone*, July 26, 1969, collected in *The Rolling Stone Interviews* (New York: Paperback Library, 1971), 212.

Medallions, "Buick '59" (Dootone, 1954).

Jess, *Tricky Cad*. See *Jess, A Grand Collage, 1951–1993*, ed. Robert J. Berthof (Buffalo NY: Albright-Knox Art Gallery, 1993), and *Made in U.S.A.: An Americanization in Modern Art, The '50s and '60s*, ed. Sidra Stich (Berkeley: California, 1987).

———, "demon-stration" (1969). Quoted in Rebecca Solnit, *Secret Exhibition: Six California Artists of the Cold War Era* (San Francisco, City Lights 1990), 38.

Wallace Berman, *Support the Revolution* (Amsterdam: Institute for Contemporary Art, 1992). Includes many Verifax collages, some in color. See also *Semina Culture: Wallace Berman & His Circle*, ed. Kristine McKenna (New York/Santa Monica: D.A.P./ Santa Monica Museum of Art, 2005).

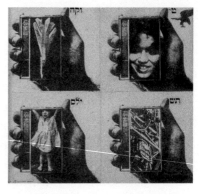

Wallace Berman, untitled, 1964

Shawn Kerri quoted in Paul D. Grushkin, *The Art of Rock: Posters from Presley to Punk* (New York: Abbeville, 1987), 442 (interview), 443 (art).

End of the Night

THE APPEARANCE OF the Doors marked a verge in the history of Los Angeles rock 'n' roll, of Los Angeles, and of the United States. That is because in their music you could hear a portent that the future, the near future, contained stories no one imagined they would want to hear, that people would not be able to turn away from, that would keep people awake, worried at the slightest anomalous sound, terrified and disgusted by their own fantasies. After Charles Manson, people could look back at "The End," "Strange Days," "People Are Strange," and "End of the Night" and hear what Manson had done as if it had yet to happen, as if they should have known, as if, in the deep textures of the music, they had.

As it was published for the first time, in 1971, before it was censored, Ed Sanders's *The Family: The Story of Charles Manson's Dune Buggy Attack Battalion* portrayed a Los Angeles that in its secret dreams imagined itself swimming in its own blood. He described a city full of people who, when they awoke on the morning of August 9, 1969, to learn that at 10050 Cielo Drive, Sharon Tate, Jay Sebring, Voytek Frykowski, Abigail Folger, and Steven Parent had been slaughtered at the house that Tate, almost nine months pregnant, had shared with her husband, Roman Polanski—slaughtered it would turn out, at Manson's direction by members of his band, Parent shot, the rest together stabbed more than a hundred times, the bodies left in cryptic postures suggesting the rituals of an unknown church—all but ran to their bathrooms to wash their hands. It didn't matter that early in the morning of the next day, the cult leader along with his followers chose at random the wealthy couple Rosemary and Leno LaBianca to kill, and smeared HEALTER SKELTER, after the Beatles song Manson had deciphered as a call to apocalypse, on their walls, or that earlier in 1969, on their album 20/20, the Beach Boys had included "Never Learn Not to Love," credited to D. Wilson/Charles Manson, or that the tune, one of many Manson had attempted to have recorded, was originally titled "Cease to Exist." The exact details of the crimes were so specifically insistent on a separate reality that people seized on them as if they were proof that, in a social sense, the crimes were not real; the desperation with which people fetishized the facts of the horror gave the denial that it had anything to do with them the lie.

Crimes far worse, less obvious, more indistinct, and more common than the singer's murder of his father and rape of his mother lay in wait in "The End"; that is why the really terrifying lines are those where the singer visits his sister and his brother, and you don't know if it's to make sure they're asleep or that they'll never wake up. But even that was too sketched in, too particular. The real caves in the performance were in hesitations, undulations of the rhythm, the full beauty in Jim Morrison's tone when he let his voice shape certain words—"nights," "die," "limitless," "hand"—or when a line he had written seemed to draw from him a confidence, a far-seeingness, that produced phrasing so lovely it could slip right past you, leaving a feeling of peace, not war: "The end of everything that stands."

In the summer of 1969, people listened again to their Doors albums, and said, *Yes, it was all there.* It was, too. Never mind the Doors of Perception. The name of the band was in the first track on its first album: "Break on Through (To the Other Side)." It wasn't a great song. For all of the contrivance of its battering rock 'n' roll momentum it was as one dimensional as an anti-war protest song. But it meant what it said, and this was part of what you were going to find when you broke down the Doors.

"The Doors really should have been at Monterey," said the disc jockey Tom Donahue on KMPX, the San Francisco FM station that had been playing *The Doors* like a commercial since its release six months before, after the close of the Monterey Pop Festival in June 1967, wondering why they hadn't been there, though in a way it made perfect sense. "This is the Love Crowd!" poor-not-yet-dead Otis Redding said during his set at the festival; the Doors were not the love crowd. They couldn't have come up with anything more harrowing than Big Brother and the Holding Company's "Ball and Chain," but Janis Joplin and her boys were nice hippies with big smiles and open hearts, even if two of them were junkies.

The weekend before the Monterey Pop Festival, the Doors appeared at the KFRC Fantasy Fair and Magic Mountain

Festival, held on Mt. Tamalpais in Marin County, an affair cobbled together by a local radio station to provide a real, San Francisco festival in the face of the Los Angeles moguls behind Monterey. The Doors appeared in the middle of the afternoon, under a bright sun, along with the Seeds, a garage band that would be celebrated in years to come for a primitive minimalism that caught the spirit of punk even before the Stooges, and Every Mother's Son, a smarmy, instantly forgotten group with a hit called "Come on Down to My Boat."

In the middle of the afternoon, the sun was still bright, but with the Doors on stage it seemed like a cloud was passing over. After the speed of the double-back beat of the Seeds' "Pushin' Too Hard," half of the numbers the Doors played seemed isolated, stranded. I don't recall if they played "End of the Night"; probably not, as they rarely did. But it's this song as much as any other that contained the history that followed, feeling for it in the dark, like a mole in the ground.

"End of the Night" could be the Impressions' "Gypsy Woman" as it opens: a descending crescendo from Robby Krieger that turns off the lights, an answering three lines from Ray Manzarek that says he was waiting for this all along. As so often with Manzarek's playing, you can hear memories of late-night TV creep-show movie marathons, or even more directly the music from early network suspense programs, and those memories are immediately transcended. As soon as you think you recognize the allusions, the music takes you somewhere else, closer to Jody Reynolds's "Endless Sleep," say, but as always slower than that, more sure, determined, fatalistic, at peace with nothing.

Within seconds, the song is underwater. Morrison swims through it, one stroke at a time, feeling the inner tides be-

tween his fingers. The descending figure from the guitar repeats until it begins to break up in a roll from John Densmore.

The heart of the performance is the way Morrison simply,
quietly chants the title of the song, four times, first in the middle of the piece, then at the end. Each time, when he sings
the phrase for the fourth time, it makes a single object that dis-
solves as he sings, as if it was never there at all, as if the clearer,
more solid first three voicings of the phrase before it were
ghosts. "End of the night end of the night end of the night end
of the night": it's a skull he can hold up to the light, until inside Blake's "Auguries of Innocence" you see "The Tiger"
plain.

| | |

A LITTLE UNDER A WEEK after the mass murders at 10050
Cielo Drive, the Woodstock Music and Art Fair: Three Days
of Peace and Music began in White Lake, New York. Had the
world known then that the butchered bodies of Sharon Tate
and her houseguests were the work of a hippie commune, a
band that would have been altogether welcome and at home
at Woodstock, the press coverage of the 450,000-strong hippie
commune that briefly established itself as Woodstock—there
were nearly as many Americans at Woodstock as, in the moment, there were in Vietnam—might not have been so ful-
some. As it was, major dailies gazed in grudging awe at the
placidity of the gathering, *Life* magazine rushed out a special
edition, and the august solemnizer Max Lerner announced "a
turning point in the consciousness generations have of each
other and of themselves." The Woodstock legend remained

inviolate and unspoiled. The Manson connection was never made. Not even the immediate, end of '69 follow-up— originally known as Woodstock West, later known as the Rolling Stones' disaster at Altamont—dimmed the magic. By 1970 the movie was playing all over the world. In 1989, demonstrators in Tiananmen Square, before they were massacred, gathered around a replica of the Statue of Liberty and told reporters Tiananmen was "our Woodstock."

The Doors weren't at Woodstock either. But they were more present at 10050 Cielo Drive, looking back from what they'd already said, trying along with everyone else to outrace the clutch of the present moment.

"End of the Night," *The Doors* (Elektra, 1967). A precious, whispery demo version from 1965, all creature-features vocal effects until a big finale, would be forgettable if it weren't for tantalizing harmonica from Ray Manzarek's brother Jim Manzarek, which hints at the song the band, still without Robby Krieger, had yet to find. See "Without a Safety Net," in *The Doors Box Set* (Elektra, 1997).

Ed Sanders, *The Family: The Story of Charles Manson's Dune Buggy Attack Battalion* (New York: Dutton, 1971); soon after publication Sanders was forced to remove a frightening chapter on the Process Church of the Final Judgement. See also the updated *The Family: The Manson Group and Its Aftermath* (New York: New American Library, 1989).

Roadhouse Blues

ONE DAY IN 2011, ZZ Top's "Sharp Dressed Man" came on the radio. Like the Doors, they get a lot of airplay on a lot of stations—though everything you hear is from one year, 1983, and one album, *Eliminator*. It's hard, funny, with Billy Gibbons's guitar as a guide to the network of caves that runs below the entire surface of the earth, even if *Eliminator* didn't have ZZ Top's best single, "My Head's in Mississippi," from 1990, which you never hear at all. That song seemed to have been conceived and sung—or, if the composer had already passed out, dreamed—with the singer's head inside a toilet bowl in a bar inevitably called the Longhorn, where the guy whose voice you hear has gone to throw up. Whether he already has or not when he first opens his mouth to get his words out, the room is still spinning, but at least he's spinning now too: he doesn't really want to be anywhere else. A naked cowgirl drifts across the ceiling of the filthy little room like a cloud. He can't believe how lucky he is.

I switched to another station, right into ZZ Top's "Got Me Under Pressure"—an *Eliminator* number a good ten times tougher than "Sharp Dressed Man." The ending, Gibbons now leaping rivers, cutting his way through mountains, is so deliriously sucked into its own crossing, cut-up rhythms it took me a moment to realize the radio had followed it without a break into another song—something that sounded so much like a ghost version of *Eliminator* I didn't immediately recognize "Roadhouse Blues."

Everybody sounded as if they were playing in each other's bands. "Roadhouse Blues" came out in 1970, the B-side of the pallid "You Make Me Real," which never broke the Top 40. Over the next forty years it became a hit, and now as it went on it felt deeper, stronger, new. Against Billy Gibbons, now pounding with his fuzz-tone guitar and fuzz-tone voice against the tin door of the bar the Doors are playing, Jim Morrison sounds hoarse.

As it led off *Morrison Hotel* in 1970, "Roadhouse Blues" was a tornado: fierce, uncompromised, fast, loud, flashy, and most of all big. You didn't have to hear the aesthetic ambition inside of it, or the desperation, the misery, chasing the charging band like a bad conscience. It was thrilling. If you were a Doors fan, you might have said, *Finally they've found their way back to their real music*, even if they'd never cut a stomp like this before. What has sustained the song over more than four decades, what has kept it reaching, is another story.

Waiting for the Sun, released in June 1968, number one, and *The Soft Parade*, released a year later and stopping at #6, the two albums that preceded *Morrison Hotel*—once past its opening blast itself a bland, vague roundelay to nowhere—were terrible jokes, regardless of who the joke was on. *Waiting for the Sun*—some mystical sun, perhaps, because in Los Angeles you don't wait for the sun, unless you're waiting for the smog to disappear, in which case you could wait forever. *The Soft Parade*—there was a wave toward a parade sound at the start, but the ruling word was soft. Both records were filled with words that had no reason to be written, much less sung. The music noodled pointlessly over broken beats, truncated melodies so ungainly most of the time Jim Morrison sounded as if he were giving a speech, and for that matter a speech less addressed to the assembled imaginary hordes of five-to-ones who were taking over than a Rotary club. "Tell All the People" opened *The Soft Parade*—"Tell All the People" not to buy this album! Robby Krieger had written the song; Morrison sounded as if he had a bag over his face, so no one would know who was singing it. There were thick-headed, battering horns all over the album, plus orchestral strings; they didn't make the music better and they didn't make it worse.

The music seemed to recognize its own pointlessness; almost everything strained, almost nothing played. At rehearsals for *The Soft Parade*, the band tumbled into six satisfying minutes circling through a teasing, pleasing melody, with Morrison shouting from far off the mike, mariachi cackling up front, the mood of a cocktail lounge where everyone in the audience is too drunk to care but the band, somehow, finds itself *interested*—like the bored, tired, disgusted bar band in *Diner* suddenly coming to life when a customer sits down at the piano and hits a glissando as if he's Jerry Lee Lewis himself. As it turned out, the Doors were playing "Guantanamero." But that wasn't on either album; it was just something that surfaced ages later on a repackaging. The truest tune on either album was "Easy Ride" on *The Soft Parade*, which was nothing if not the Doors' equivalent of Elvis Presley's "Do the Clam," legendary as the worst record he could make, if only conceptually—and who could get past the concept? Could anybody make a worse record? The Doors were trying; you could hear the self-loathing coming out of the songs like sweat, if that was your idea of a good time. Really, what were *Waiting for the Sun* and *The Soft Parade* but the Doors' versions of Elvis-movie soundtracks like *Roustabout* or *It Happened at the World's Fair*?

There was one number that didn't fit, that seemed to exist on some other album. On *Waiting for the Sun* "My Wild Love" was a forest chant, more distant, receding farther into the past, with each wordless, doubled *Huh huh huhn*. It breathed the same pagan smoke as Josef Škvorecký's "Emöke," where at a Czech health resort a man encounters a woman carrying the soul of someone who knows how to worship trees. At three minutes, "My Wild Love" was infinitely more experimental than the seventeen-minute phallic-environmental "Celebration of the Lizard," recorded as an "experimental work in progress" at the time, performed on stage in 1968, but not released until long after the band was gone. With "My Wild Love" you couldn't place where you were, you didn't know where you were going, but you could feel it was somewhere neither you nor the musicians had been before. Burrowing into itself, into the old European forest, the day darker with each step, this was a hint, like the first page of a fairy tale in a book where the rest of the pages have been torn out, of an untold story, the promise of a journey that might go on indefinitely, the chant revealing its forest, the forest generating its own chant. Where did this song come from? On these albums, patently nowhere, though you could hear fragments of the tales it didn't tell hiding in "The End" and "When the Music's Over." Where did it go? Into "Roadhouse Blues."

Early on during the first day in the studio, on November 4, 1969, with the band trying to cut the song, Krieger's rolling fuzz-tone opening, the bare skeleton of the rhythm, is there for a fragment called "Talking Blues." "Me and my baby walking down the street," Morrison drawls, sounding like that's exactly what he's doing. "We's being friendly to every person we meet / Say, hi, neighbor, how you doin'? / Hey, Dylan, how you doin'"—as if they'd just passed each other on the cover of *The Freewheelin' Bob Dylan*, one of Morrison's favorite albums. But for the first named take of "Roadhouse Blues" there is again that riff and nothing else. The rhythms are all sprung; as Krieger pushes ahead, with energy, with ambition, he falls behind his own beat. Everything is off, but there's a sense of purpose: *There could be something here if we could find it.* "The point was to work completely in the dark," George Grosz said of his life as a dadaist in Berlin after the First World War; the challenge was to make the darkness. Stumbling, that's where they're headed.

Perhaps casting back to a night at the Whisky when Them followed the Doors' lurching "Back Door Man" with their own death race through "Baby Please Don't Go," that's the song Morrison is now singing, or singing around. It's a signpost, a pointer. He falls into nonsense words, syllables bumping into each other, but it's an attempt to find the beat that won't reveal itself, to sucker it into giving them at least the outline of a song. There's a guitar solo, out of place. Morrison begins a verse he has, "Woke up this morning"—but he backs off from it, as if he's embarrassed by his own words, or ashamed. It's a purely blackface vocal—"Well, ah woke up this moanin'"—and he all but hides from it, his voice slurring against itself, the sound of someone singing with his mouth closed. He goes back to words that aren't words, sounds that in the finished song might be

Beep a gunk a chucha
Cronk cronk cronk
You gotta eatch you puna
Eatch ya bop a lula
Bump a kechonk
Ease sum konk

But here the whole, long passage is nothing remotely transcribable, a race against language for its own sake: the sake of the race, not language. Speak in secret alphabets—Morrison was calling himself a poet, but what if he could? Poetry wants to begin from the beginning of language, or before it, to use ordinary words as if no one has heard them before. Is this what was happening in the third take of the song? Whatever it was, the Doors hadn't heard themselves speaking that language before, closer to glossolalia than a device, sound that sings the body, cutting the mind out altogether. As the broken, backwards words unwound like a string of DNA, the band was back in the forest, reaching for its chants.

That first day, they keep hammering at the door of the song. There are times when they sound like a bar band, after hours, no one else around. The rhythm is never of a piece, but there are moments when something that is not quite a song, that might be more than a song, is present, like an apparition; then it's just another stumble. Every time that last verse, "Woke up this morning," comes around, Morrison backs away from it; why does he keep singing it?

The next day the setting is different. Lonnie Mack, the great Indiana blues guitarist known for his 1963 version of Chuck Berry's "Memphis"—an all-instrumental pursuit of every shading of rhythm in the song, opening up what in Berry's hands might have seemed a simple if oddly stuttering piece of country music into a labyrinth of dreamy complexity—had recently signed to Elektra. He was around; the Doors asked him to play bass. The band likely didn't know his soul ballad "Why," one of the most dramatic and painful American songs ever recorded—by the last verse, a heart attack the singer survives to his regret—but they knew they were in the studio with a man who, as the Mississippi blues singer Skip James once said to a gushing fan, had been and gone from places they would never get to. But they had been and gone from places Lonnie Mack would never get to, too. They had to live up to each other.

Over and over, Morrison—who could be in a gauzy nightclub or on Elvis's bare stage, accosting passersby on the street or buttonholing hangers-on in the studio—is going on about how "Money beats soul, every time." He seems to have made this part of the song—or to be using the line and its costuming—"Ladies and gentlemen, on this stage, for the first time in the Western world, we have: money beats soul, every time"— to keep away the song he has to sing, make, find, prove.

Maybe because of Mack's presence, or the leaping pace he helps set, for the first time the inner size of the song, its rhythmic scope, begins to take shape. The beat is hard for the first time. Krieger still cannot bring the guitar into the rhythm, but on his own there's freedom all over his playing, and soon he's flying. "Oh, I woke up"—still there is something morally wrong with these lines, there is something in them that pushes Morrison away from his own words, and he sings with no conviction, as if it's a bad dream.

Again, Morrison dives for a monologue—there are two songs here, and one will have to play itself out before the other can speak in its own voice. "Money beats soul," he states over a nightclub piano, the lounge singer after ten too many requests for "Stardust," drunk but forming his words carefully in the belief there's someone left in the place he can still fool. He croons: "I-got-something-to-tell-you-about-your-soul." He stops crooning. "Your soul ain't worth shit. You know how much your soul's worth? Your soul's worth about as much as you can get on Wall Street, my dear. Now, you may think I'm cynical, or dangerous, to tell you that. You may think that I'm, ah, a little hard to take—*hey*—listen, doll, I'll tell you the goddamn truth"—and he garbles his words like his mouth is full of pebbles—"Money beats soul, every time." There is more of this.

Once more, "Roadhouse Blues." John Densmore is now giving the music a bounce it didn't have before. His sound is all will—a sound, somehow, that can't be taken back, each beat a step on a journey you can't retrace. There's a confidence in Krieger's guitar playing that lifts the music, that gives everyone a plane to rise to. Morrison is shouting his words, cleanly: "Keep your eyes on the road, your hands upon the wheel"—with *wheel* pulled down, creating a sense of jeopardy, the use of the formal *upon* throwing the story out of the present, into some past-future where the rules won't be what you're used to, whatever they are. Krieger goes off on long, lucid runs, a tremendous presence. Morrison drifts back to

"Baby Please Don't Go," but only for a moment, as if to get his bearings as he asks the band to slow down, to wait.

In the performance that was released, the music is all slices, knives cutting into the song, each penetration leaving it stronger, bigger, more a thing itself, impervious to any error. It's a simple story. There's a roadhouse. People go there to get drunk, to have a good time, to find each other. There are cabins out back. The command at the start of the song is so deep, so earned, it almost makes you squint as you listen, as you keep your eyes on the road, keep your speed steady, to get there before it's too late and the band has packed up and the cabins are full. The drumming holds the song together as the guitar goes in one direction, the singer in another. "Musically, as a guitar player, Robbie is more complex," Morrison said earlier in 1969. "—like, chord changes, beautiful melodies and that—and my thing is more in a blues vein: long, rambling, basic and primitive." Never as the Doors played would those two sides exert a greater, more sympathetic tension than for this performance. Every instant is a whole song: a story, found on the spot, beginning in the middle, that feels completely open, a story that could break in any direction. Out of nowhere comes a chant: "SAVE OUR CITY! SAVE OUR CITY!"

In Pittsburgh, on May 2, 1970, for the fourth number of the set, the band hammers into the song. It will take them seven minutes to tease, demand, threaten the song to force it to give up every secret it was made to reveal, and the drama unfolds when Morrison, his voice already desperate, preternaturally full, expanding with each line, descends into the bubbling swamp of the tune, the place without words. He disappears into the maw of the music and keeps going, *you gotta cronk*

cronk cronk sh bomp bomp cronk cronk cronk eh hey cron cronk
cronk ado ah hey che doo bop dag a chee be cronk cronk well
rah hey hey tay cronk cronk see lay, hey — he sustains it all for a
solid minute. It's harder than it looks. With each measure of
vocal sounds the pressure is increased, the pleasure is deeper,
the abandon more complete, the freedom from words, meaning, song, band, hits, audience, police, prison, and self more
real, precious, and sure to disappear around the next turn if
you don't keep your eyes on the road. In that long minute,
Morrison sings the whole song in another language, one only
he could speak, but that anyone could understand. There is
no document he left behind where he sounds more fulfilled
as an artist, as someone who threw down a gauntlet and said,
to himself, to you, to whoever was listening, to whoever
wasn't, follow *that*.

| | |

WHEN THE DOORS RECORDED "Roadhouse Blues" in November 1969, Morrison's arrest in Miami the previous March,
the three months of concerts cancelled everywhere in the
country that followed, the felony trial looming in the next
year, the likelihood of prison, and after that the end of the
band, were only the most obvious demons. The specter of the
Manson slaughter hung over every Hollywood icon, hanger-
on, or rock 'n' roll musician as if it were L.A.'s Vietnam.
Everyone — people who had been in Manson's orbit, like Neil
Young, or anyone who knew someone who knew someone
who had, which was everyone — believed there was a hit list,
held by those Mansonites waiting patiently, on the outside, for

the word of the messiah. There were reasons to believe that the Manson bands were just a first brigade—a lumpen avant-garde, you could say—for a web of cults biding their time for years, since the late 1940s, some said, when the British sex-magick maven Aleister Crowley, John Parsons, the founder of the Jet Propulsion Laboratory, and L. Ron Hubbard practiced Satanist rituals in Pasadena, determined to summon the whore of Babylon and conceive a living Antichrist.

Drink, dread: Morrison did not need more than Manson, or for that matter whatever Hollywood flophouse he was sleeping in on any given night, to keep drinking. He had been a drunk for years—at any time a more determined, violent, serious, re-flective, incompetent, untrustworthy, unbearable degenerate drunk than his friends, his girlfriend, or the other members of the group had seen before. "How about . . . feel like discussing alcohol?" Morrison said to Jerry Hopkins in the summer of 1969. "Just a short dialogue. No long rap. Alcohol as opposed to drugs?" An interview where the star is asking the writer for permission to discuss something he cares about? When does this happen? "Getting drunk . . . you're in complete control up to a point," Morrison said. "It's your choice, every time you take a sip. You have a lot of small choices. It's like . . . I guess it's the difference between suicide and slow capitulation." "What's that mean?" Hopkins said. "I don't know, man," Morrison said, then ending the interview with a showman's flourish: "Let's go next door and get a drink."

All of that was in "Roadhouse Blues": not as autobiography, not as confession, not as a cry for help or a fuck you to who-ever asked, but, as Louise Brooks liked to quote, she said, from an old dictionary, "a subjective epic composition in which the author begs leave to treat the world according to his own point of view." Finally, for the master take of the song and almost always afterwards, the last verse of the song came through in its own voice. There was still a tinge of blackface, but no embarrassment. These were the most painful, resolute lines in the song as they were sung—the most convincingly fatalistic lines in the Doors' career.

"After the war," a friend once said of the quiet, brooding British spy novelist Eric Ambler, whose pre-war heroes were ordinary Englishmen caught up in the breeding fascist hegemony of Europe in the 1930s, and whose post-war thrillers were merely complex entertainments devoid of moral stakes, "he must have lost his sense of dread." What the Doors rediscovered in "Roadhouse Blues," what again they found a way to voice, was not any particular style, any return to fundamentals, basics, roots, but the language of dread that drove *The Doors*—not words, but the way words are sung, turned, examined as they shoot by, the way they work like title cards for musical passages, which is where the language speaks.

At first they seemed melodramatic, even self-pitying: "Well, I woke up this morning, and got myself a beer / Well, I woke up this morning and got myself a beer / The future's uncertain and the end is always near." Morrison bore down on *beer* both times. He let the last line hang in the air, tossing it off like a weather report. It wasn't his death that made the verse stick, that made everything else in the song a road meant to take you to precisely this spot. It was more than forty years on the air, the song keeping up with the times, the song moving on as if it had seen and then countenanced every new twist in history in advance, the song not defeated or reduced or softened by time but matching it beat by beat, step by step.

ZZ Top, "My Head's in Mississippi" (Warner Bros., 1990).

"Push Push" (aka "Guantanamera"), bonus track on *The Soft Parade* (1969) (Elektra, 2006).

Elvis Presley, "Do the Clam" (RCA, 1964, #21). From *Girl Happy*, and best heard on *Elvis' Greatest Shit!!* (Dog Vomit bootleg, 1984). Co-written by Dolores Fuller, who in 1953, in Ed Wood's *Glen or Glenda*, handed the transvestite director the angora sweater he craved beyond all flesh. "Turn and tease, hug and squeeze / Dig right in and do the Clam"—how far is that from "Touch Me"? Pretty far, if you accept the double entendre.

"My Wild Love," *Waiting for the Sun* (Elektra, 1968).

Josef Škvorecký, "Emöke" (1963), included in *The Bass Saxophone* (New York: Knopf, 1979).

"Celebration of the Lizard," bonus track on *Waiting for the Sun* reissue (Elektra, 2006).

"Roadhouse Blues" outtakes, November 4, 1969, "Talking Blues," takes 1–3, 6; November 5, take 1; "Money Beats Soul," takes 13–15. Bonus tracks on *Morrison Hotel* (1970) (Elektra, 2006).

Lonnie Mack, "Memphis" (Fraternity, 1963, #5). Included with "Why" on *The Wham of That Memphis Man!*, reissued by Elektra in 1969 as *For Collectors Only*. For "Why," see GM, "Songs Left Out of Nan Goldin's *Ballad of Sexual Dependency*," *Aperture* (Winter 2009). Also guesting on "Roadhouse Blues" on November 5 was John Sebastian, late of the Lovin' Spoonful, brought in to overdub blues harmonica that cut through the song like a runaway horse. He was credited as G. Pugliese—to avoid "the fine print of his solo-artist deal with Reprise Records," according to the liner notes to the 2006 *Morrison Hotel* reissue. John Densmore: "Years later Paul confirmed my suspicions that back then John, like some of the public, was embarrassed by the Doors. Sebastian didn't want to be associated with the group. The backlash that had started with us changing our precious Doors sound by using an orchestra on our fourth album had

escalated with the Miami incident, and it was still in force"—
even though if he'd used his own name Sebastian probably still
would have gotten to sing "Welcome Back, Kotter." Densmore,
Riders on the Storm: My Life with Jim Morrison and the Doors
(New York: Delta, 1991), 236–37.

Jim Morrison, on music, Jerry Hopkins, "The Rolling Stone Interview," *Rolling Stone*, July 26, 1969, collected in *The Rolling Stone
Interviews* (New York: Paperback Library, 1971), 221.

——, On alcohol, as above, 232–33.

"Roadhouse Blues," Pittsburgh City Arena, May 2, 1970, *Live in
Pittsburgh 1970* (DMC/Bright Midnight/Rhino, 2008).

"You Make Me Real"/"Roadhouse Blues" (Elektra, 1970).

Queen of the Highway

DEPENDING ON HOW you hear it, this is Bill Murray's nightclub sleazeball Nick Winters, strolling from table to table, weaving the words of whatever standard or current hit he's singing into the same, all-purpose drool he's dripping over newlyweds or vacationers or businessmen-with-hookers or ready-to-divorce-on-the-spot couples kept only by their own politeness from strangling him on the spot ("'Lost in a Roman wilderness of pain,' hey, we've all been there, right?")—or it's the latest of the countless lounge singers who always kept two copies of *Chet Baker Sings*, one LP to play, one still shrink-wrapped, pristine, to gaze at, to hold, to walk around the room with while listening to the other one, murmuring "I Fall in Love Too Easily," "But Not for Me," "My Funny Valentine." Or it's a walk away from a career already suspended over a void of nothingness, it's almost any cut on an album that's meant to pretend it's just a song, not a worthless, desperate bet against ruin. On *Morrison Hotel* in 1970, this song—these words and this melody—comes across as the work of musicians who don't trust themselves. Whenever the song seems about to speak, it's broken up, all but attacked, by melodramatic stops, screeching effects; whatever charm the singing might have is given over to histrionics as soon as a mood threatens to exert its own gravity, its own pull on the story—to cover words like "princess" or "meadow" with regret over chances never taken.

But there is another version of the song. Fooling around in the studio, with John Densmore treading lightly, seemingly waiting to make a move even as he does so, with session-man Harvey Brooks on bass and Ray Manzarek dropping down into an afterbirth-of-the-cool piano fantasy—Manzarek is playing without thinking, without feeling, the same runs he's used in this song or a hundred others a thousand times before, with no more soul or any less, the music of someone who has nothing else to do, nothing else he can do—fooling around, Jim Morrison can ignore the Doors, their triumphs and their mistakes. He can ignore his bandmates and himself. He can ignore their audience, whatever it might be, and pretend it doesn't exist, that it never did, or that soon enough it won't.

He and the others in this moment can pretend the band never existed, that instead of picking up a guitar player and shopping their 1965 demo, recorded at World Pacific studios, where Chet Baker himself had recorded, they'd stayed right where they were, a why-not? signing by the little jazz label—and though the Ray Manzarek Quartet never got further north than Santa Barbara or east of Bakersfield, playing Ross Macdonald country until every road actually looked different, there were those jam sessions after hours, on Sunday afternoons, that no one ever forgot. Like the day, after weeks of *I don't know, if it's cool, man*, Baker really did show up, everybody whispering, even though the word was later that he'd only been there because somebody said it was a connection? That too-beautiful 1950s face already cracking and shriveling, cheekbones like scaffolds? And the tone that came out when he sang, *Not real*, someone said, even though it was as if it wasn't there at all? They can pretend that, or they can pretend that after the Doors crashed, two or three of them would show up, unannounced, at the Ruby Red or the Piano Stick, to do that weird slow version of "Light My Fire"—"This is how I always heard it," Morrison would say to the crowd, half a dozen tables and the people at the bar—and then "Queen of the Highway," this way, so smoothly, the singer with his eyes closed, so at ease with himself that words like "monster" floated out from under his tongue like something he'd already forgotten, all the ideas about theater, the pronouncements about art and chaos, the ambition to be different, to make a difference, all the sense of a verge in time different from any other, all the public meetings, bled out for good, and good riddance.

"He was the exact opposite of his friend Art, who put everything of himself into every note he played," Geoff Dyer writes of Chet Baker. "Chet put nothing of himself into his music and that's what lent it its pathos."

The music he played felt abandoned by him. He played the old ballads and standards with a long series of caresses that led nowhere and subsided into nothing.

That was how he had always played and always would. Every time he played a note he waved it goodbye. Sometimes he didn't even wave.

That was something to aspire to. "Queen of the Highway," as it came to life one afternoon, Densmore tapping his way through the song as he, Brooks, and Manzarek look for its mandated, clichéd, satisfying cool-jazz close, was a wave, but at least whatever it was waving to was no longer there.

"Queen of the Highway," *Morrison Hotel* (Elektra, 1970).

———, outtake from *Morrison Hotel*, from "Without a Safety Net," in *The Doors Box Set* (Elektra, 1997).

Geoff Dyer, *But Beautiful: A Book About Jazz* (1991) (New York: Picador, 2009), 132. See also Dave Hickey, "A Life in the Arts," in *Air Guitar: Essays on Art & Democracy* (Los Angeles: Art Issues Press, 1997), and James Gavin, *Deep in a Dream: The Long Night of Chet Baker* (2002) (Chicago: Chicago Review Press, 2011)—which, as a biography, is not just one thing after another, like most biographies, but as the biography of a junkie, the same one thing after another, and, somehow, in Gavin's hands, with every same thing different.

Take It as It Comes

YOU COULDN'T CONJURE UP a more stark example of a song whose music runs away from its words—carries them away, runs them to the edge of a cliff, and throws them off.

As one of the first numbers the Doors recorded, it comes on like a conventional rock 'n' roll song, or as close to a conventional rock 'n' roll song as anything else the Doors did, which was not all that close. In 2009 the compilers of *Where the Action Is! Los Angeles Nuggets 1965–1968*, a four-CD collection of singles from the likes of the Leaves ("Dr. Stone," their drug song), the Standells ("Riot on Sunset Strip"), Sonny and Cher ("It's Gonna Rain"), Captain Beefheart ("Zig Zag Wanderer"), and dozens of others, found it sufficiently conventional to sandwich it with the Association's "One Too Many Mornings" (their Dylan cover), the Knack's "Time Waits for No One" (not that Knack, and not the Rolling Stones song from seven years later), Kaleidoscope's "Pulsating Dream" (which unfortunately tried to live up to its title), and the Seeds' "Tripmaker" (their drug song). But the archivists had to compress the sound, bleed out the bass, turn up the treble, make the sound tinny, small, and itchily complaining, like everything else, to make the Doors fit, and it didn't work anyway.

Like everything else on *The Doors*, "Take It as It Comes" came out of the box big, full, breathing its own air. Unlike anything else, it seemed to start in the middle of some greater song, opening at top speed, too fast to even turn around to see where the song came from. As a sheet of words it was little more than a quick, cut-down version of the Byrds' shimmering cover of Pete Seeger's "Turn! Turn! Turn! (To Everything There Is a Season)" — "A time to live, a time to die" — from 1965, a gorgeous, inescapable number one hit. If anyone had played "Turn! Turn! Turn!" as a lead-in to "Take It as It Comes," the Doors' version would have erased it, made its reach and joy feel pious and fey. If the two songs were the Stingray and the XKE on Dead Man's Curve, the Byrds' black 45 would have been a grease spot.

Robby Krieger too begins in the middle, the middle of "Turn! Turn! Turn!" — with the same glow the Byrds' gave their sound, the same lyricism, the sense of lightness and beauty, beauty as an idea, a concept, something less to create than to quote. But almost before his gesture can register, John Densmore is pressing, pounding, rounding a turn and coming out of it so fast he pulls everyone with him. In an instant the chorus has arrived and everything coming out of Krieger's guitar is percussive, assaultive, matching Ray Manzarek's high, flooded runs through the song. From that point, everyone has the music in their hands; they can do anything with it at any moment.

"Time to live, time to lie / Time to laugh, time to die": with eerie composure—as if he's been doing this at least as long as Mick Jagger and is only now hitting his stride—Jim Morrison is singing words about how it's necessary not to rush, not to push, to be careful, to hold back, walk don't run. But he takes flight with his first line, an Icarus leap, and the words are either a joke or a dare, the singer daring the listener to believe a word he says. *Don't move too fast if you want your love to last,* he sings, with his hands on the wheel, his foot to the floor, and his eyes squeezed shut.

Halfway through the bare two minutes of the song—though so much is happening so quickly that when the song is over it can seem to have been playing for two, three times as long— the band pulls back. Compared to the cacophony of the moment before, the song is almost silent, just Manzarek's bass device counting off time, the effect not of the song moving forward slowly, but the music in complete suspension. This is a conventional device—the old "Whole Lotta Shakin' Goin' On" trick, the "Shout" trick—but it feels completely new. Instead of a roadhouse with a screaming crowd suddenly holding its breath, it's midnight on a beach, the waves are almost silent, the sky blue-black, the moon bright enough for faces and close enough to touch. Just like that, you want the song to stay here. You don't want it to go back on the highway. You don't want to move at all. You only want to— And then, much too quickly, a house falls on the music and you can't remember that the song had ever stopped, that there was anywhere to go but straight ahead, straight into a wall if that's what's there.

Nearing the end—and again, if someone stopped you, pulled you aside, and said, *Do you realize all this has been happening in about 110 seconds, Jerry Lee Lewis needed three minutes, the Isley Brothers almost five*, you'd say, *What, what?*—it's all fury, frenzy, Morrison's leap in the first seconds of the song now little more than hesitation. "Specialize in having fun," he says, but whatever it is that's happening now, it's much bigger than anything such a sentiment could touch. There's too much at stake. Too much has been left behind. *You've been moving much too fast*, Morrison chants in the last words of the song, when everything the music—the drums, the organ, the guitar, his voice—has told you that you're moving much too slowly, that you're standing still, that you haven't begun.

"Take It as It Comes," *The Doors* (Elektra, 1967).

Where the Action Is! Los Angeles Nuggets 1965–1968 (Rhino, 2009). Featuring paint-thinner vocals, crinkly sound, guitars that are supposed to chime but don't, Peter Fonda's "November Night," such forgotten or hard-to-believe-ever-existed bands as the Common Cold and Pasternak's Progress, Gene Clark's altogether unconvincing "Los Angeles" ("city of doom" he sings, as if someone else wrote it and he's wondering what doom means), a pathetic cover of Sonny Knight's 1961 deep-soul classic "If You Want This Love" by the West Coast Pop Art Experimental Band, "Marshmallow Skies," Rick Nelson's sententious attempt at psychedelia, and "Back Seat '38 Dodge," inspired by Edward Kienholz's notorious, still-shocking life-size, or rather death-size, 1964 assemblage, which the Long Beach quartet Opus 1 turns into a little horror movie: "What's in the back seat of my '38 Dodge? I really want to know." But even the unanswerable Jackie DeShannon's

"Splendor in the Grass," recorded with the Byrds, promises more than it delivers. No wonder the producers had to squeeze the Doors to get them through theirs.

Byrds, "Turn! Turn! Turn!" (Columbia, 1965).

The End, 1968

WHEN JIM MORRISON SAID that a Doors concert was a kind of public meeting, it was December 14, 1968, hours before the band set up in the L. A. Forum before 18,000 fans. "It was a big deal for us," Robby Krieger said years later. "Local band plays where the Lakers play!"

By the end of 1968 the Doors were a Top 40 band. Their last two singles were number one and #3—though they would never again make the top ten. This night they were planning mostly songs from *The Soft Parade*, still more than six months from release. They had a string sextet, a horn section, and thirty-two amplifiers on the stage. There were three opening acts: Tzon Yen Luie, a Japanese koto player; the cloying Los Angeles group Sweetwater; and Jerry Lee Lewis. All were booed as if they were impostors. "I hope you have a heart attack," Jerry Lee told the audience. When the Doors came on, there were cheers, but quickly the crowd was drowning out the music with chants for "Light My Fire"—which, for once, the band was determined not to play. Unable to get their new music into the air, they gave in—and as soon as they were finished the crowd began to chant for "Light My Fire" again. "Cut out that shit," Jim Morrison said. He looked out and asked a question as if he truly did want to know the answer, as if he had no idea what it might be: "What are you all doing here?" He began to taunt the crowd with the same lines that would crack open the show at the Dinner Key in Miami three months later: "You want music?" Everybody screamed. "Well, man," he said, "we can play music all night, but that's not what you really want—you want something more, something greater than you've ever seen, right?" In Miami, in a drunken rage, those words would suddenly mean that he should show the crowd his penis, that if only symbolically, because it was his, it would be something greater than anyone had ever seen. In Los Angeles the words hung in the air and someone shouted "We want Mick Jagger."

Finally, with the show breaking down, Morrison went to the edge of the stage and in an oracular voice began to declaim "The Celebration of the Lizard." He stopped. People laughed. He went on: "One morning he awoke in a green hotel. With a strange creature growing beside him." "Is everybody in?" he asked, then again, and again, with each time people shouting: "NOOOOOO!" "The ceremony is about to begin," he said portentously—try saying the words any other way—and people laughed out loud at the pomposity of it all, or giggled in embarrassment. Then Morrison stood silently. It went on. "Stupid," someone mutters. "Asshole!"

"WAKE UP!" Morrison screamed. The band crashed down around him. Many long minutes later, it ended. "When it ends he glares at the audience," one report had it, "no words need be spoken, and he walks off to almost no ovation." "You give people what they want or what they think they want and they'll let you do anything," he would say the next year, looking back and seeing clearly. "But if you go too fast for them and pull an unexpected move, you confuse them. When they go to a musical event, a concert, a play or whatever, they want to be turned on, to feel like they've been on a trip, something out of the ordinary. But instead of making them feel like they're on a trip, that they're all together, if instead you hold a mirror up and show them what they're really like, what they really want, and show them that they're alone instead of all together, they're revolted and confused. And they'll act that way."

It was a sometimes excruciating performance, sometimes confusing and alive, the band bashing atonally, refusing any rhythm, Morrison singing and reciting and roaring and whispering—and on *Boot Yer Butt!*, a strange four-CD collection that the remaining Doors released in 2003, it's just one more spectral, all but illusionary moment in a waking-dream account of the band's career, from their earliest live recordings, from a show at the Avalon Ballroom in San Francisco in March 1967, to the last city save one in which they would ever step on a stage. "Our record album is only a map of our work," Morrison had said of *The Doors* in 1967, though as a record album it was as close as they got; this is the territory.

Beginning with "Moonlight Drive" and the band's cover of Howlin' Wolf's "Back Door Man," ending almost four years later, this meandering walk down an endless beach—you can see people carrying bulky tape recorders and extension mikes following the four guys in the Doors as they walk through the sand, their bootleg mission not to let a random sigh or curse escape — is not drawn from soundboards or well-made audience tapes. It is a compilation of absolutely horrible recordings made with damaged equipment and originally pressed into illegal vinyl that warped and splintered as soon as you tried to play it. On these recordings, Morrison can sound miles and miles away from the little handheld microphone that's picking up his messages, messages that sometimes feel as if they're coming from the bottom of a well. You may not be able to make out a single instrument behind his voice — or, even more displacingly, you may hear one instrument only. The band can emerge and disappear, as if it's playing a séance, not a show. You can listen to the entire set straight through, more than forty performances collected or, really, smeared together, and then start all over again, trapped in its faraway, incorporeal spell, and part of that spell is the drama that emerges as the spool unwinds: the drama of a band at war with its audience.

In the beginning, you hear discovery and embrace: an audience embracing a band, a band's embrace of its audience, but most of all a band's discovery and embrace of its own music — a band's laying claim to music that, whatever its legal status as something they owned, might have still been beyond their reach in a manner they could not deny. The way they find their way into "Break on Through" at the Continental Ballroom in Santa Clara, California, on July 9, 1967 — the way they break through the song — is a storming assault. Hundreds of soldiers are climbing the stairways of a once-impregnable fortress and burning it down from the inside — but not before they stop to gaze upon the wonders of the place, the arching ceilings held up as if by mere air, the walls as thick as horses, the marble floors, the gargoyles in the eaves. They dance in a circle, and then, as the fire begins to rise, they only dance faster. No one here gets out alive, Morrison would announce two years later in "Five to One," but this performance begs that cheap song's question: who would want to?

A few months later, at the Swing Auditorium in San Bernardino, on December 16, Morrison is falling all over "Alabama Song," losing the words, the song slithering away from him in disgust. The shows become erratic. With "Light My Fire" drawing fans who don't care if they hear anything else and often enough are drunk enough, or stoned enough, to take anything else as an insult, a rebuke, at best what they have to put up with to get what they want, there is an edge of contempt in the halls, though it isn't obvious where it's coming from.

Morrison reached for the skies. A version of Muddy Waters's "I'm a Man" at Winterland in San Francisco, on December 26, is expansive, open, churning, with Morrison and the band improvising long, slow vamps around a sing-songy speech about taking over the world—something, as Morrison digs into the music, the song itself is suggesting. Isn't that what a man is supposed to do? Does the song say there are any limits to what a person can do? That's the last thing it says. With the grunge of gray, mottled, echoing sound around him, Morrison is raving as if he is the first to discover what the song always wanted to say, because he has discovered the nerve to say it.

It all blows up in Miami, but there is anger breaking out well before. In Amsterdam, on September 15, 1968, Morrison collapsed after swallowing drugs in order to get through customs; Ray Manzarek ended up singing every song, turning the Doors into a bar band covering Doors songs. Everywhere, the distance between the band and its audience is thrown into relief, perhaps more symbolic than—night to night in any given town—real, by the distances in the sound itself: the way the music is muffled, as if the band is playing behind a curtain, the singer in front, except when he grabs it in the middle and drapes a length of it over his face.

The set proceeds chronologically, except for the very last song: "The End," from the Singer Bowl, in Queens, New York, on August 2, 1968. Because any version of the Doors' career had to end with "The End"? Because nothing could follow these bizarre, ugly seventeen minutes?

Robby Krieger's insinuating guitar line is clear; the little filigree he plays turns the song over. The crowd is loud, drunk, screaming. "Come on, Jimmy!" shouts a man. "Jimmmmyyyy-ayyyyyy, light my fire!" screeches a woman. She sounds like someone running through an asylum while orderlies with syringes try to bring her down. "We just did that one," Morrison says reasonably. There's an organized chant, five or six people shouting together: "Come on light my fire!" "Hey," Morrison says, sounding a little surprised. "This is serious." There's more yelling. "SSSSHHHHHHHH," Morrison whispers.

"Fuck you!" someone shouts.

The sound now muffled, his words unintelligible, Morrison tries to talk through the rising noise. "Hey, it ruins everything," he says. "SSSSHHHHHHHH," he says again. The band keeps time behind him. More than two minutes have gone by and they haven't been able to start the song.

"This is the end," Morrison sings, clearly, the sound picked up loudly. The crowd is silent, but Morrison sounds distracted, as if he's losing faith in the song: losing faith that it's worth singing. "You'll never follow me," he sings. "In his face!" someone screams. Morrison tries to sing but he can't find the song. His voice turns oratorical. The woman in the insane asylum is rushing all over the hall, and you can't tell if she thinks she's on stage or that the people on stage are trying to kill her. Morrison improvises lyrics that turn into doggerel. People seem to respond in kind: "MORRISON IS IN HIS CAVE!" "UP WITH MARTIANS, DOWN WITH—" if that's really what anyone is shouting.

Morrison—the band is barely present now—tries to float over the noise, but the scratch of the woman's voice, a sound that feels like someone is tearing her nails down your face, makes it impossible. You're getting to know these people, this small knot in the cauldron of the recording standing in for everybody else. It's a mosh pit where sounds do all the slamming. People are screaming parodies of the lyrics that Morrison isn't singing. In the murk he has more presence than ever—but the huge, godlike voice is nothing compared to the far more powerful, mocking crowd.

Morrison is again making up words for the song, to throw the crowd off, to summon the song from the dead: "A creature is nursing its child, soft arms around the head and the neck, a mouth to connect, leave this child alone, this one is mine, I'm taking her home, back to the rain"—he sounds like a cowboy stuffed with books. There are long, unintelligible passages from Morrison, and then the image of the rain carries through the static of the audience and out of nothing a story shoves itself forward.

"Stop the car," Morrison says, plainly; it's a film noir set piece. "Rain. Night"—he lets loose a muffled scream. He could be in *Detour*, the killer driving straight out of the ditch with the body in it, which in this moment is in Queens, which is worse. "I'm getting out. I can't take it anymore. I think there's somebody coming." He half sings: "There's nothing you can *do* about it."

There is silence; the band isn't playing, for a second no one is talking, or yelling. The moment is so anomalous the silence seems absolute. Someone screams something about cake. The madwoman screams—every scream from her is the same. If she were just a face you could look away. In the back of his mind, a story Morrison would tell a friend the next year is already there. "I went to a movie one night in Westwood," he'd say, "and I was in a bookstore or some shop where they sell pottery and calendars and gadgets, y'know . . . and a very attractive, intelligent—intelligent in the sense of aware and open—girl thought she recognized me and she came to say hello. And she was asking me about that particular song. She was just out for a little stroll with a nurse. She was on leave, just for an hour or so, from the UCLA Neuropsychiatric Institute. Apparently she had been a student at UCLA and freaked on heavy drugs or something and either committed herself or someone picked up on her and put her there. Anyway, she said that the song was really a favorite of a lot of kids in her ward. At first I thought: Oh, man . . . and this was after I talked with her for a while, saying it could mean a lot of things, kind of a maze or a puzzle to think about, everybody should relate it to their own situation. I didn't realize people took songs so seriously and it made me wonder whether I ought to consider the consequences . . ."

"The killer awoke before dawn," Morrison says stiffly. He seems to rush the song, as if he wants nothing more than to get this part of it over with. The band is still not there. "He took a face from the ancient gallery," Morrison announces. "And he walked on down the hall," several male voices answer him. "And he walked on down the hall," Morrison says, as if they've reminded him of what he's supposed to say. "WALKED ON DOWN THE HALL!" the woman screams. You can't tell if he's taunting the crowd or taunting himself, because he knows every word will come back at him, stupid grins on the faces of the people in the crowd, "And he walked on down the hall" now a punch line to something that didn't start out as a joke. The band is vamping behind him. "Father," Morrison says. "Yes, son," a guy in the crowd answers. "YES SON!" answers the woman. "I want to kill you" says a man from the audience. "I want to kill you," Morrison repeats without expression. He tries to take the song back: "Moooootherrrr—"

Screams rise up as if out of the ground, without human agency. "I . . . want . . . tuh—" The band speeds up, then stops. There are strangled sounds out of Morrison's throat, he tries to shout, the crowd is quiet, Morrison is speaking in words that aren't words, as if he's trying to explain the song to himself. He sings in self-parody, then locks into sounds inside the words, sounds as demented as those anyone in the crowd is making. His voice is over here and his body is over there. Then the crowd is screaming at him in a way that hasn't happened before: in the face of the screeching, crows flying out of people's mouths, you can see Morrison as the people in the crowd are seeing him, a freak, the Elephant Man, the crowd thrilled at how grotesque he is, how crazy, everybody pointing, and though the band is playing, now the real music is coming from the crowd, a tangled skein of sound moving through the hall without a brain.

There are crashing sounds from the band, then from the crowd, we're-all-going-to-die-and-I-can't-wait sounds. It's scary. Anything could happen except anything good.

Morrison tries to sing the end of the song; he does, but all of his trust in the song is gone. Someone in the audience puts two fingers in his mouth and blows. He does it again.

It all comes to an end. You've listened to all four discs, for more than five hours, mesmerized. You can start over. You can't imagine that the group could have. You remember that this is a false ending, that the chronologically last song of the set, "L.A. Woman" from the State Fair Music Hall, in Dallas, on December 11, 1970, was all shadows, figures disappearing into the mist, a singer trying to find the face that would explain everything, and maybe succeeding. You can't believe the band pushed on that far, that long. They were tougher, maybe, or as Charlie Poole sang in "If I Lose, I Don't Care," in 1927, four years before he drank himself to death, "The blood was a-runnin', I was running too / To give my feet some exercise, I had nothing else to do."

Boot Yer Butt! The Doors Bootlegs (Rhino Handmade, 2003).

Jim Morrison, "You give people what they want," from Jerry Hopkins, "The Rolling Stone Interview," *Rolling Stone* (July 26, 1969), collected in *The Rolling Stone Interviews* (New York: Paperback Library, 1971), 229.

——, "only a map," from "The New Generation: Theater with a Beat," *Chicago Tribune*, carried in the *San Francisco Chronicle*, September 28, 1967.

——, "I went to a movie," from Hopkins, 225–26.

Charlie Poole, "If I Lose, I Don't Care" (Columbia, 1927). For the country inside one of the most American songs America has ever produced, see the anthology *"You Ain't Talkin' to Me": Charlie Poole and the Roots of Country Music* (Columbia, 2005); for the soul, Loudon Wainwright III, "If I Lose," on *High Wide & Handsome: The Charlie Poole Project* (2nd Story Sound, 2009).

Light My Fire, 1966/1970

IN THE STUDIO IN 1966, the song took shape in two parts: the first half, through Ray Manzarek's solo, and the second half, running Robby Krieger's solo through to the final choruses and then the end.

It's all of a piece. All across Manzarek's solo there is a beast to one side, John Densmore, who with the constant, pushing insistence of tumbling drums, could be eating the music whole, spitting it back. At unexpected moments he pulls back, pulls Manzarek with him, his sound suddenly full of open spaces, and you hear a stick hit the snare as a single event. With Krieger's solo he is more circumspect, as if the beast isn't sure what species of animal it's now faced with, as if it's willing to wait to find out. As the passage goes on, so fluidly from

Krieger, Densmore repeats the single snare shot he used to kick the song off, the first thing you hear, its echo immediately swallowed by Manzarek's opening fanfare—and, at the end, almost the last thing you hear. From start to finish, Densmore's hand is on the wheel; that is why everyone else sounds so free.

Following not Krieger's original composition but Ray Manzarek's mad-scientist lab work, the whole performance is one great circle. The tale—like a founding story, Moses with his tablets, Fred C. Dobbs with his lottery ticket—has been told so many times, acted out bit by bit in Oliver Stone's *The Doors*, because it's a good story.

Just off the beach in Venice, the band is trying to find its music. Morrison has some songs; nobody else does. Like a high school teacher, he gives everyone an assignment: come back with a new song. Only Krieger does: a verse and a chorus. "I was trying to do something that was reminiscent of 'Hey Joe,'" he said years later, "the version by the Leaves"—an L.A. band whose principal distinction was that they were likely the first of far too many groups to record "Hey Joe," and possibly the least convincing. For a song about a man killing his unfaithful lover, the Leaves sound like they're playing with matches. But they did have a bright sound and they played fast. Krieger's ambition revealed the germ of trash and chart-chasing at the heart of the high, churchlike seriousness of the band at its most distinctive, for better or for worse: Krieger was trying to write a hit. Why else write songs?

It didn't take anyone long to realize it was a song. As Morrison came up with the second verse, rhyming "mire" with "pyre," both words were too literary, too far from the ordinary language of the pop song, to have been on Krieger's mind. But then came the part of the story that made it a story, and made the song something more.

Manzarek thought the music needed a frame, a kicker, something to seal it—something that would let the listener pull it out of the air, something that would let the musicians put it there. Go out to the beach, he said. Leave me alone while I figure it out. He gives a technical explanation:

> All my classical studies came to fruition. A simple circle of fifths was the answer. The chords were G to D, F to Bb, Eb to Ab (two beats on each chord), and then an A for two measures. Run some Bach filigrees over the top in a turning-in-on-itself Fibonacci spiral.

"Like," he said, now a poet, someone trying to get you to see what he heard, "a nautilus shell." You can hear him tell Krieger, Morrison, and Densmore exactly that, and sooner than later the music taking exactly that shape—a closed but continual Möbius strip neither musicians nor listeners could escape, something so right, and so unlikely, it almost made no sense.

Announcing itself, announcing the song, announcing the band just after Densmore's first drumbeat, the piece Manzarek devised is thrilling—thrilling as a promise, thrilling as a thing in itself. If the song itself wasn't so eager to say everything all at once, you'd linger over Manzarek's fanfare, wanting to hear it again; it would block the song. But you forget it.

Morrison sweeps through the first verses and choruses like a visitation, a magic carpet on its way to somewhere else, and Manzarek steps into his solo. There is something cheesy, something all but ? & the Mysterians about his sound—to one ear, the tinny, trebly organ never varying, but to the other ear never boring, textures and shifts of tone and points of view always changing, fast, impossible to track, a car rushing up and down the canyon roads, then out on the Pacific Coast Highway in the middle of the night, a Porsche Spyder, Jan and Dean's woodie, a zebra-striped hearse, from beginning to end anything with a motor and four wheels. Both ears are hearing the same thing at the same time.

When Krieger appears, just after three minutes, it's a surprise, because you've forgotten there's a guitar in the music. Anonymously chording all through Manzarek's solo, as unvaryingly as the bass piano Manzarek uses to plant the rhythm, Krieger has disappeared from his own song, and when he emerges, it's more than a surprise, it's a shock. This is man-on-horseback music, all grandeur, nothing rushed, as stately as a marble staircase, a full-size copy of *The Winged Victory of Samothrace*, or Eric Clapton's solos in "All Your Love" and "Spoonful": that close to white elephant art, close enough to the immortal to stay on the air for its lifetime without one note ever predicting the next.

In Honolulu, in April 1970, the band spent almost twenty-one minutes in the song. When Krieger stepped in after seven and a half minutes, he turned it toward "My Favorite Things"; two minutes later he was playing hard, searching for a pulse the song might have always hidden, and at twelve minutes he was still flying. He was reclaiming his song; at this point, you've forgotten that Jim Morrison too was ever part of it, and so it's a shock in turn when, after more than fourteen minutes, Morrison returns, as if from limbo, or backstage, or the men's room, to turn the song again, this time into "Fever," then "Summertime," then the Doors' own "Love Hides."

But in 1966, in the studio, there is no accounting for Krieger's hold on the music: the lines he is crafting are so sonically clear, so emotionally transparent, that when he cuts into a fast flurry of notes it's as if the whole edifice is about to crack. Then the flow is back, the coast highway now stretching into the night farther than you can see or even imagine, Manzarek is surfing behind Krieger, Manzarek's shifts and slides appearing and disappearing seemingly without will or intent, carried by Krieger's waves, a great smile, all pleasure, loose in the water, and you might wonder: How can this ever end? How can they get out of this? How will they ever get back to the song? It's like seeing a movie you've seen a hundred times before and still not believing that what happens next will, that you can't change it, that you can't stop the shot, the slamming door, the fall from the bell tower.

They get back with Krieger pulling up short, as if at a roadblock; it's the only jarring moment of the song. But as Krieger stops, John Densmore increases the speed, and soon everyone has followed him over the crest of the music, right into the arms of Manzarek's shining shell, no longer a fanfare, but a confirmation that life is not the same, terrain has been crossed, and the day won't end as it began. *Something is about to happen*, that roll of organ chords said at the start; *something has happened*, they say now.

At the beginning, in the studio, in the first verses, there's an echo on Morrison, creating a hollow, reverberating effect, so that he feels bigger than life, floating above the action, all knowing, all seeing. Smooth, full, rounded, not a crack or a tear, it's not a blues voice, not a rock 'n' roll voice, perhaps closer to Dean Martin's than anyone else's, if Dean Martin could ever bring himself to the pace of "Light My Fire." But now, at the end, with the verses and choruses repeating, Morrison too has made the journey, and when he returns with "The time to hesitate is through," you believe this isn't just a line he's spouting, or using; he's learned that it is true, and his goal, for as long as the song remains his, is to explain how and why this is so. He does it with physical force, pressing on the words, the melody, pulling the organ, the guitar, the drums toward him, until finally at the end his voice can tear.

Densmore again hits his snare, a single beat, but harder, cleaner, than the sound that began the song. Manzarek follows one more time with the little circle the performance has followed, expanded, from the start. It is the most satisfying ending imaginable: it doesn't leave you wanting more. It leaves you shaking your head in delight.

"Light My Fire," *The Doors* (Elektra, 1967).

——, Honolulu Convention Center, April 18, 1970, collected on *Boot Yer Butt! The Doors Bootlegs* (Rhino Handmade, 2003).

Robby Krieger and Ray Manzarek, in *The Doors with Ben Fong-Torres, The Doors* (New York: Hyperion, 2006), 43.

Leaves, "Hey Joe" (Mira, 1966, #31).

Eric Clapton, "All Your Love," on John Mayhall with Eric Clapton, *Bluesbreakers* (Deram, 1966).

——, "Spoonful," on Cream, *Fresh Cream* (Reaction, 1966).

Epilogue:
"You're Not Going to
Be Remembered"

WHEN ACTORS MIGRATE from movie to movie, traces of their characters travel with them, until, regardless of the script, the setup, the director's instructions, it's partly the old characters speaking out of the mouths of the new ones, guiding a new character's hand into a gesture you remember from two or twenty years before. This transference can be immediately unsettling: Joan Allen and Tobey Maguire as mother and son in 1997 in *The Ice Storm* and in *Pleasantville* barely a year later make each movie a version of the other, and each character a version of the people who, as you watch, the actor and actress are playing somewhere else. *Don't they remember?* you almost say out loud in the theater as Maguire's David tries to get through to Allen's Betty Parker in *Pleasantville,* and the answer is, they do—not just the actors, but the characters.

As Harvey Keitel moved on from his first role in Martin Scorsese's 1968 *Who's That Knocking at My Door,* through Scorsese's *Mean Streets* in 1973, his *Taxi Driver* in 1976, James Toback's *Fingers* in 1978—Keitel's best and most extreme performance, seemingly folding everything before and after into a single Jimmy as he breaks into pieces—all the way to Abel Ferrara's *Bad Lieutenant* in 1992, to Quentin Tarantino's *Pulp Fiction* in 1994 and on from there, the roles aged Keitel in the strongest manner. He thickened, even coarsened, over the decades; his flesh slipped, his skin went dull, but his eyes burned more brightly when he was old than when he was young. Even playing himself in the stupid finale of *Get Shorty* in 1995, he seemed to carry all of his past roles with him, somewhere in the back of his mind, in the fatigue or in the vehemence of his gestures—and also, in those flinty eyes, the viewer's own memory of those roles. The uncanny appears: with this double memory in play, Keitel moves and speaks as if he is conniving with himself, playing what we haven't seen him do yet against what we've seen him do before.

But the uncanny gains in resonance the farther the echo is from its source. In *The Doors,* in 1991, Val Kilmer's Jim Morrison is drunk on a plane with his road buddy Tom Baker, played by Michael Madsen, an actor who, when you watch him now, no matter what his role or when the movie was made, always seems to be doing a version of his Mr. Blonde razor dance to "Stuck in the Middle with You" in *Reservoir Dogs*. It's March 1, 1969; Morrison and Baker are on their way to the Miami concert that will upend the Doors' career. Baker looks over at Morrison's belly, which seems to be ballooning as we watch. "What are you going to do when the music's over?" he says, Madsen's face revealing the slightest embarrassment over the telegraphed self-referentiality of the script. But his face retrieves a sense of the real for the next line: "You're not going to be remembered, Jim." And so after dying in the bathtub in the last scene of the movie Kilmer's Morrison migrates through nearly a score of roles—an uncredited, out of focus dead Elvis in *True Romance*, an unsuccessful Bruce Wayne in *Batman Forever*, barely noticed as Doc Holliday in *Tombstone* or barely seen as Simon Templar in *The Saint*, part of the scenery as Willem de Kooning in *Pollock*, until finally, with Jim Morrison the one part still burned onto Kilmer's face, he turns up again in L.A. in 2003 in Bob Dylan's *Masked and Anonymous*, scars or scratches down his cheeks, long hair, a loose beard, now herding sheep and goats in a tiny encampment in a parking lot, sharpening a big knife, ranting about God and man and corruption and vanity, all but automatically mouthing *What have they done to the earth? What have they done to our fair sister?* from "When the Music's Over."

In 2003 it's more than twenty years since the journalist Jerry Hopkins and the Doors insider Danny Sugerman, in their enormous best-seller *No One Here Gets Out Alive: The Biography of Jim Morrison*, cynically hinted that despite their title Jim Morrison wasn't dead after all: that, like Elvis, he'd faked his death to escape the pressures of fame, not to mention the real possibility of prison, where anything could happen, but that he'd be back, that one day—* It's been twenty years since the one-time Sixties generational historian James Howard Kunstler, picking up Hopkins's and Sugerman's cue, published his equally cynical novel *The Life of Byron Jaynes*, where at the end the Jim Morrison character shows up naked on a motorcycle. It's been twenty years since Jim Morrison lookalike Michael Paré, playing the long presumed dead singer Eddie Wilson, shows up at the end of the film *Eddie and the Cruisers*, in the midst of an Eddie and the Cruisers revival, to see his younger self in a bank of TV screens in the window of an electronics store, only to walk away alone, his

---

*On December 9, 2010, on the initiative of outgoing Governor Charlie Crist, the Florida Clemency Board granted Morrison a pardon for the convictions resulting from his 1970 trial for indecent exposure, public obscenity, and inciting to riot. On December 22, John Densmore, Robby Krieger, and Ray Manzarek issued this statement:

"In 1969 the Doors played an infamous concert in Miami, Florida. Accounts vary as to what actually happened on stage that night.

"Whatever took place that night ended with The Doors sharing beers and laughter in the dressing room with the Miami police, who acted as security at the venue that evening. No arrests were made. The next day we flew off to Jamaica for a few days' vacation before our planned 20-city tour of America.

"That tour never materialized. Four days later, warrants were issued in Miami for the arrest of Morrison on trumped-up charges of indecency, public obscenity, and general rock-and-roll revelry. Every city the Doors were booked into canceled their engagement.

"A circus of fire-and-brimstone 'decency' rallies, grand jury investigations and apocalyptic editorials followed—not to mention allegations ranging from the unsubstantiated (he exposed himself) to the fantastic (the Doors were 'inciting a riot' but also 'hypnotizing' the crowd).

shoulders hunched, a lovely, satisfied look on his face. If Val Kilmer's old mirror man is going to show up anywhere, isn't it more likely, isn't it more right, that it'd be as a half-crazy Nature Boy in a dystopian future Los Angeles ruled by Third World gangsters than as Byron Jaynes's Joe Doaks in New England or Eddie Wilson's Mr. No Name in New Jersey? "A crack in the mud at the bottom of a sun-dried lake I count more beautiful than any human being, you know what I mean?" says Kilmer's animal man, sounding as if he's quoting from a book of Jim Morrison's poetry, as Bob Dylan's Jack Fate looks on impassively. "Know what you mean," Dylan says. "Kinda like a curse on being born." "You got that right," says Kilmer. "That's 'cause we live in fear. 'Cause we know we're going to die." He picks up a rabbit. "Animals don't know

---

"In August, Jim Morrison went on trial in Miami. He was acquitted on all but two misdemeanor charges and sentenced to six months' hard labor in Raiford Penitentiary. He was appealing this conviction when he died in Paris on July 3, 1971. Four decades after the fact, with Jim an icon for multiple generations—and those who railed against him now a laughingstock—Florida has seen fit to issue a pardon.

"We don't feel Jim needs to be pardoned for anything.

"His performance in Miami that night was certainly provocative, and entirely in the insurrectionary spirit of The Doors' music and message. The charges against him were largely an opportunity for grandstanding by ambitious politicians—not to mention an affront to free speech and a massive waste of time and taxpayer dollars . . . If the State of Florida and the City of Miami want to make amends for the travesty of Jim Morrison's arrest and prosecution forty years after the fact, an apology would be more appropriate—and expunging the whole sorry matter from the record. And how about a promise to stop letting culture-war hysteria trump our First Amendment rights? Freedom of Speech must be held sacred, especially in these reactionary times."

they're going to die," Morrison says, stumbling over his words, his thoughts backing up in his head, with "The End" and "People Are Strange" and "L.A. Woman" and even "Alabama Song" backing up too, all of it coming out in the mindless voice of someone who regardless of who might be standing in front of him is always talking to himself, or God. "Holds us back, knowledge of death. I say, amazing grace indeed," he says, as he raises his knife.

The Doors, directed by Oliver Stone, written by Randall Jahnson and Stone (1991).

Masked and Anonymous, directed by Larry Charles, written by Sergei Petrov (Bob Dylan) and Rene Fontaine (Larry Charles) (2003).

Jerry Hopkins and Danny Sugerman, *No One Here Gets Out Alive: The Biography of Jim Morrison* (New York: Plexus, 1980).

James Howard Kunstler, *The Life of Byron Jaynes* (New York: Norton, 1983).

P. F. Kluge, *Eddie and the Cruisers* (New York: Viking, 1980).

Eddie and the Cruisers, directed by Martin Davison, written by Davidson and Arlene Davidson (1983).

Acknowledgments

This book was fun to write, and part of the reason why is that, over the years, writing about the Doors and others here and there, I was lucky to find people who were fun to work with: Lisa Bralts-Kelly at *Cake* in Minneapolis, Danny Alexander at Johnson County Community College, Nancy Duckworth, Jon Carroll, and Bill Broyles at *New West/California*, Doug Simmons at the *Village Voice*, David Frankel and Ingrid Sischy at *Artforum*, Graham Fuller at *Interview*, Bill Wyman at *Salon*, Steve Perry and Melissa Maerz at *City Pages* in Minneapolis, Mark Francis at the Centre Pompidou, Michel Braudeau at *la Nouvelle Revue Française*, the staff of the Seattle and Portland Arts and Lectures series, Hal Foster at Princeton, Vendela Vida and Andrew Leland at the *Believer*, Eric Weisbard at the Experience Music Project, and Melissa Harris at *Aperture*. I owe thanks to Ben Fong-Torres and Jerry Hopkins, for their invaluable work on the Doors and their friendship over many years, and as well to Kathi Goldmark, Joel Selvin, Dave Marsh, Michael Sragow, Tosh Berman, Kristine McKenna, Erik Bernstein, and Tabitha King.

At PublicAffairs I was privileged to work, again, with my editor Clive Priddle, publisher Susan Weinberg, Melissa Raymond, Jessica Campbell, Tessa Shanks, all-seeing production manager Christine Marra, copy-editor and fact-checker Gray Cutler (what errors remain are not hers), Jane Raese and Pete Garceau for their spare and clean designs, indexer Donna Riggs, and, at Faber & Faber, again, with my editor Lee Brackstone, Helen Francis, Anna Pallai, and Ruth Atkins. Wendy Weil of the Wendy Weil Agency, with Emily Forland and Emma Patterson, and their associates Anthony Goff and Georgia Glover at the David Higham Agency in London, always make life easier.

This book began with nights my wife Jenny and I spent at the Avalon Ballroom in San Francisco, waiting for the Doors to come on. We took handbills on the way out, and for some reason, over five houses in forty-four years, they never disappeared.

Illustration Credits

Index

Greil Marcus is the author of *Bob Dylan by Greil Marcus, Writings 1968–2010*, *When That Rough God Goes Riding*, and *Like a Rolling Stone* (all three with PublicAffairs), *The Old Weird America*, *The Shape of Things to Come*, *Mystery Train*, *Dead Elvis*, *In the Fascist Bathroom*, and other books; a twentieth anniversary edition of his *Lipstick Traces* was published in 2009. With Werner Sollors he is the editor of *A New Literary History of America*, published by Harvard University Press. Since 2000 he has taught at Berkeley, Princeton, Minnesota, NYU, and the New School in New York; his column Real Life Rock Top 10 appears regularly in the *Believer*. He lives in Oakland, California.

PublicAffairs is a publishing house founded in 1997. It is a tribute to the standards, values, and flair of three persons who have served as mentors to countless reporters, writers, editors, and book people of all kinds, including me.

I. F. Stone, proprietor of *I. F. Stone's Weekly*, combined a commitment to the First Amendment with entrepreneurial zeal and reporting skill and became one of the great independent journalists in American history. At the age of eighty, Izzy published *The Trial of Socrates*, which was a national bestseller. He wrote the book after he taught himself ancient Greek.

Benjamin C. Bradlee was for nearly thirty years the charismatic editorial leader of *The Washington Post*. It was Ben who gave the *Post* the range and courage to pursue such historic issues as Watergate. He supported his reporters with a tenacity that made them fearless, and it is no accident that so many became authors of influential, best-selling books.

Robert L. Bernstein, the chief executive of Random House for more than a quarter century, guided one of the nation's premier publishing houses. Bob was personally responsible for many books of political dissent and argument that challenged tyranny around the globe. He is also the founder and was the longtime chair of Human Rights Watch, one of the most respected human rights organizations in the world.

. . .

For fifty years, the banner of Public Affairs Press was carried by its owner Morris B. Schnapper, who published Gandhi, Nasser, Toynbee, Truman, and about 1,500 other authors. In 1983 Schnapper was described by *The Washington Post* as "a redoubtable gadfly." His legacy will endure in the books to come.

Peter Osnos, *Founder and Editor-at-Large*

JUNE 2 THU FRI
THE MILLER
BLUES BAND
DAILY FLASH

JUNE 3 SAT 4 SUN
DOORS
THE MILLER
BLUES BAND

AVALON BALLROOM

SUTTER & VANNESS · DANCE · CONCERT · SAN FRANCISCO
LIGHTS · NORTH AMERICAN IBIS ALCHEMICAL CO.

TICKET OUTLETS - SAN FRANCISCO: KWASIDIKA (HAIGHT-ASHBURY), CITYLIGHTS BOOKS (N.BEACH) KELLEY GALLERIES (3681-A SACRAMENTO), THE TOWN SQUIRE
1318 POLK) BALLY LO SHOES (UNION SQ), HUT T-1 STATE COLLEGE. BERKELEY: MOES BOOKS, DISCOUNT RECORDS. SAUSALITO: TIDES BOOKSTORE
REDWOOD CITY: REDWOOD HOUSE OF MUSIC (700 WINSLOW) . SAN MATEO: TOWN & COUNTRY MUSIC CENTER (4TH & EL CAMINO), LA MER CAMERAS &
MUSIC (HILLSDALE AT 19TH). MENLO PARK: KEPLER'S BOOKS & MAGAZINES (825 EL CAMINO). SAN JOSE: DISCORAMA (235 S. FIRST ST).

FD 64-1   1957 © FAMILY DOG PRODUCTIONS 639 GOUGH ST., San Francisco, Calif. 94102